Praise for *The Transformation of a Man's Heart*

"Finally, someone has written a book that deals with the 'real' issues that men face. *The Transformation of a Man's Heart* is not just another men's 'how to' book but rather a book that deals with who men are at their core and what transformation looks like from the inside out. This book is a great read for men individually and will be a wonderful tool for men to go through in a small group. If you are a man, then this is a must read."

STEVE SONDERMAN, ASSOCIATE PASTOR OF MEN'S MINISTRY AT ELMBROOK CHURCH, BROOKFIELD, WISCONSIN, AND FOUNDER, TOP GUN MINISTRIES

"As a connoisseur of men's books, I have never seen a better collection of insights and encouragement by men, for men. It's full of straight talk about the real stuff. For anyone who ponders the uniqueness of a man's experience of life, this is a must-read book."

PAULA RINEHART, AUTHOR, *STRONG WOMEN, SOFT HEARTS*

"Warning to men who may read this: Enter into the pages of this book only if you are willing to have your heart transformed and begin to become the man that God has created you to be."

DR. CHUCK STECKER, PRESIDENT/FOUNDER, A CHOSEN GENERATION

"Some books are compendiums of knowledge holding promise to teach us, and these are good. Others—a rare few—are crucibles of wisdom brimming with power to change us, and these are best. This is such a book. Steve Smith has gathered a company of warriors and sages, wounded healers all, to distill their hard-won insights about things human and things divine, and then pass it onto us. My only caution: if you're happy skimming the surface of your own life, content with dabbling in the shallows, don't read it. It's bent on taking you deep."

MARK BUCHANAN, AUTHOR, *THE REST OF GOD*

"*The Transformation of a Man's Heart* is a fantastic book of powerful messages, communicated with great effectiveness. This is a book for those who long to change—both in heart and in character—and know that lasting change doesn't come easy. I so appreciated the honesty from this group of men, and they have become 'accountability partners' for me, encouraging deeper intimacy with God and my family. It will deepen your understanding, enrich your faith and guide you through the transformational changes you will want to make."

LIEUTENANT GENERAL R. L. VANANTWERP, U.S. ARMY

THE TRANSFORMATION OF A
MAN'S HEART

COMPILED AND EDITED BY

STEPHEN W. SMITH

IVP Books

An imprint of InterVarsity Press
Downers Grove, Illinois

InterVarsity Press
P.O. Box 1400, Downers Grove, IL 60515-1426
ivpress.com
email@ivpress.com

InterVarsity Press® is the book-publishing division of InterVarsity Christian Fellowship/USA®, a movement of
students and faculty active on campus at hundreds of universities, colleges and schools of nursing in the United States
of America, and a member movement of the International Fellowship of Evangelical Students. For information about
local and regional activities, visit intervarsity.org.

Design: Cindy Kiple
Images: Fredrik Broman / Getty Images

ISBN 978-0-8308-2145-7

Printed in the United States of America ∞

Library of Congress Cataloging-in-Publication Data

The transformation of a man's heart / edited by Stephen W. Smith.
 p. cm.
 Includes bibliographical references and index.
 ISBN-13: 978-0-8308-2145-7 (pbk.: alk. paper)
 ISBN-10: 0-8308-2145-7 (pbk.: alk. paper)
 1. Christian life. I. Smith, Stephen W., 1954-
BV4501.3.T72 2006
248.8'42—dc22

2006005553

P 19 18 17 16 15 14 13 12 11 10 9 8 7 6
Y 21 20 19 18 17

CONTENTS

OUTWARD

FORWARD

FOREWORD

Imagine sitting around a table with a group of men who have agreed to meet with you to share the stories of their own spiritual journeys. Taking you over the terrain they have traveled. And taking you there with unflinching honesty. Showing you not only the sunshiny vistas but the shadowy valleys. With the sharp rocks underfoot and the steep drop-offs on the side. Telling you where they have stumbled, where they have fallen. And telling you also what brought them to their feet and put them on a path that led to the transformation of themselves as men.

Imagine those conversations, and you have a good idea what *The Transformation of a Man's Heart* is all about. It's a bringing together of men to talk about subjects ranging from failure to father wounds, from sex to spiritual friendships, from leading a family to leaving a legacy.

My good friend Steve Smith sets the tone for the book in the very first chapter with how transparently he talks about the transformation of his *own* heart. This book is full of stories. Some will make you think. Others will make you cry. Still others will make you kneel. All will make you want to be a better man.

The story of Steve's conversation with his son will *open* your heart.

The story of Julian Lennon will *break* your heart.

The story of the man going to his father's gravesite will *inspire* your heart.

Together, they will *transform* your heart.

Or at least they will start the process. As the book says, transformation is never finished this side of heaven. Still, it is never too late to start. Or too early. And I can think of no better place to start than with the book you are now holding in your hands.

Ken Gire
Author of *Moments with the Savior, Windows of the Soul,*
The North Face of God

ACKNOWLEDGMENTS

The Transformation of a Man's Heart was birthed out of need—not just my own need but the deepest longing of nearly every man I have ever met. If we get lost while driving in a city, we refer to a map to find our way. But where is the map to help us find how to be a man and experience authentic transformation?

Men need help to find their way. The twenty-first century appears to be littered with the carnage of the lives of men who have tried to change in a hundred different ways, yet failed. The residue on the hearts of many men today is thick; we are left to live in shame, blame and guilt over our failures and repeated mistakes.

This is not a book crammed with tips and techniques. Rather, this is collection of stories by men who share their hearts, lives and longings for authentic transformation. Choosing the contributors was like participating in the draft of the National Football League. IVP gave me the opportunity to take this vision and find twelve male voices who could speak from experience and passion to men today and in future generations.

It is a privilege to know most of these men personally and to count them as companions on my own journey. The few that I've not yet met were guiding voices for me in their writings. Their lives and messages converge within these pages to offer the reader a guidebook rich with Scripture, honesty, candor and longing. Hopefully, their collected voices will become a guiding conversation on our journey to become transformed Christian men.

InterVarsity Christian Fellowship has played a large, vital, shaping role in my understanding of what it means to be a Christian man. I found Jesus Christ on my college campus through InterVarsity, became president of my InterVarsity chapter and attended its Urbana Missions Convention as a college sophomore. Little did I know as I read the pages of J. I. Packer, John Stott, Paul Little and other authors of IVP books that one day my own voice would be heard through InterVarsity Press. This has, in every way, been a humbling experience.

I want to express my gratitude to Dallas Willard, who at one of my lowest moments as a man and minister convinced me that transformation was indeed possible. Those three weeks in the monastery in southern California changed my life forever. I arrived burned out and in desperation; I emerged different and have never looked back. Thank you, Dallas, for speaking into my heart and for believing.

Without any question, my own journey toward transformation has been enriched and deepened by the companionship of men who sought the same things I so longed for: deep change that would last and intimacy with God. Some of these men I found in the church; others found me. Among these are Steve Metcalf, Vance Brown, Tim Harris, Mike Deets, Brian Marcotte, Col. Paul Meredith, Tim Oakley, Chuck Millsaps, Rick Campbell, Ray Walkowski, Michael Doyle and Craig Glass. To each of you, my deepest thanks for sharing a part of the journey with me.

Dave Zimmerman, my editor, helped me shape this book when it was but clay deep in the pit of my heart. Dave's work was more than with words on paper. It was like having a friend who knew the way when I was lost, deep in the forest. My special thanks to Cindy Bunch, senior editor at InterVarsity Press, for believing in this vision when I first shared it.

The passion to keep going and see this project to completion was stirred by my own four sons who so need a book like this. As I worked late into the night on this, they and their hearts are what made me want to do this. I see their struggle, and I want them to hear from some other men who struggle just like they do but who are winning. Thank you Blake, Jordan, Cameron and Leighton! Your hearts are on the journey and I hope this book will greatly help you find the way for a long, long time.

My wife, Gwen Harding Smith, stood by me each step of the way. There is no other heart on Earth who has wanted this message or my own transformation more than you. You make me want to be transformed.

Stephen W. Smith
Potter's Inn at Aspen Ridge
Divide, Colorado

1

TRANSFORMATION

UNDERSTANDING THE PROCESS

Stephen W. Smith

Man looks at the outward appearance,

but the LORD looks at the heart.

1 SAMUEL 16:7

At age thirty-four years, I was called to be the senior pastor of a large, thriving church in a southern city. This was a "megachurch in the making," complete with four Sunday worship services, scores of deacons and the "greatest staff ever called to serve." Moreover, I was the leader. My suite of offices looked palatial, with mahogany credenzas, a huge desk and heavy crown molding.

I felt a sense of entitlement in this new position. For ten years I had kept to a relentless schedule, working my way through several churches, each with more members, larger budgets and greater prestige than the last. All the while my eyes had been on the prize—pastoring a large church. And now my dream had come true!

At the zenith of my career, I invited Gary Chapman, author of *The Five Love Languages* and contributor to this book, to lead a citywide conference based on his book and themes. During his presentation, Gary guided us in identifying our own "love language." The conference was hugely successful and just one more recognition for our church.

After Gary's last service, my wife, Gwen, served a wonderful Sunday dinner to our family. While savoring our meal, I began to hurriedly "check in" with the family. After all, I had to return to church in two hours for a leadership meeting. We planned to announce our proposal for a bigger sanctuary.

Our dinner became more like a business meeting as I probed Gwen for how she thought Gary did and what responses she had heard from our congregation. She suggested I ask our sons. Evidently, some discussion had already taken place prior to my arrival at home.

Starting with Blake, our oldest son, then ten years old, I asked, "Did you enjoy Dr. Chapman today?"

"Why yes, yes I did, Dad," Blake replied haltingly.

"Do you happen to know which love language you have?" I probed, glancing at my watch, mindful of the upcoming meeting.

"Yes, Dad, I do know my love language. My love language is time, and *you* never give me any."

My son's words devastated me. His disappointment in our relationship was clear. Hadn't I always wanted to be such a good father? My own father was devoted to his work and provided well for our family. But I always yearned for more of Dad's time. Now Blake confronted me with the same problem—father hunger. Ten years had gone by and I hadn't made time for my sons or my wife.

Guilt consumed me. Reflecting more on Blake's words, I began to see myself for what I had become—a sort of driven machine that showed up and sprinkled "pastor dust." Although I hoped my presence would make occasions better, I wasn't real any more. I had neglected the price that one pays for deep relationships—time, balance and connection to God.

I had no strength or desire to hide behind a façade any longer. I could no longer ride the waves of success and significance wreaking havoc throughout my family, world, friends and heart. This wake-up call proved a sacred epiphany—my opportunity for transformation.

BETWEEN A ROCK AND A HARD PLACE

The journey toward transformation is all about reshaping our hearts, not the muscle within our chest but what Henri Nouwen calls "our hidden center."

> We know little to nothing of our spiritual heart. We keep our distance from it, as though we were afraid. What holds the passion inside of us is what frightens us most. Where we are most ourselves, we are often strangers to ourselves. That is the painful part of being human. We fail to know our hidden center and our submerged parts and so we live and die without knowing who we really are. If we ask ourselves why we think, feel and act in a certain way, we often have no answer, thus proving to be strangers in our own house.[1]

Recently, I sat with a military officer and his wife. This career officer, conditioned by years of training to hide emotion, sat stoically at attention with his wife in front me. The wife began to speak in a frustrated and sadly defeated tone: "I can't take it any more. To live with Mike, well, it's like . . . it's like living with a rock. I can't get through. He is so tough on the outside. But I don't think there's *anything* on the inside." She continued, "All I want is his heart. I want all of him. But he won't give it to me."

His wife was going to leave him. He wouldn't be with his children. His outer life was disintegrating and his inner life was in turmoil. What was I going to say? "Read a book about renewing your marriage? Have a ten-second kiss each morning and evening? Take fifteen minutes to ask about each other's day?" This man needed to journey deep within himself to discern his heart and share what he found with his wife.

RENOUNCING DENIAL

The journey to transformation begins with the desire to look at and own the truth about myself. It continues as I face the *larger* truth that I'm unable to permanently change myself without the power of God. If I could have, I would have. Nothing short of this sincere desire for change will launch us on the path toward transformation.

A good mirror shows us truth. But we have to look into that mirror. We must *seek* to *find*. A mirror's reflection reveals the truth about every man. Can we really cover things up? Can a well-made, tailored jacket cover forty-five extra pounds? Can a quick smile cover the rage we just expressed? Can warning the family that "We don't talk about this outside this house" hide the lurking dysfunction?

One evening in the middle of the night, Bill's wife caught him staring into the computer screen in the basement office. Bill had escaped there to enter the dark hole of cyber pornography. Once confronted by his wife through angry tears, Bill promised to "never do it again." He meant it too. He was almost relieved. Bill wanted to return to his values.

Yet, within days, Bill secretly slipped off to the basement after making sure his wife was asleep to revisit—just this once. He wrestled with guilt yet returned again and again. Bill was held in the clutches of false intimacy, unreal women and selfish desires. Soon, he justified his need for this gratification and pronounced it one of his little secrets. He simply couldn't stop.

Most of us have lived long enough that we have no interest in judging Bill or interpreting his actions. We realize that life as a Christian man simply doesn't work like a logarithm in a math class. Indeed, we know our *own* slippery places, and we know that solemn promises often don't stick. Our old friend self-reliance often lets us down.

A friend confessed in a men's group I led recently, "Steve, I *need* transformation because I know what it is like *not* to be transformed." My friend succinctly stated what is true for us all. We yearn for real change, and we know we can't do it alone.

I DON'T HAVE WHAT IT TAKES

Jesus and John the Baptist announced the kingdom of God with the words "Reshape your lives, because God's new order of the Spirit is confronting you" (Matthew 3:2; 4:17 *Cotton Patch Version*).

Reshaping our lives involves picking up a reliable mirror and looking squarely at ourselves—above and below the surface. Paul's words in Romans 7:18-24 model this kind of reflection for us.

I realize that I don't have what it takes. I can will it, but I can't *do* it. I decide to do good, but I don't *really* do it; I decide not to do bad, but then I do it anyway. My decisions, such as they are, don't result in actions. Something has gone wrong deep within me and gets the better of me every time.

It happens so regularly that it's predictable. The moment I decide to do good, sin is there to trip me up. I truly delight in God's commands, but it's pretty obvious that not all of me joins in that delight. Parts of me covertly rebel, and just when I least expect it, they take charge.

I've tried everything and nothing helps. I'm at the end of my rope. Is there no one who can do anything for me? Isn't that the real question?" (*The Message*)

Paul's honest admission leaves little room for blaming others, making excuses or complaining about his lot in life. Instead, this biblical passage shows an honest man, without excuse, holding up the mirror of self-reflection. I wish we were all this honest.

At the revelation that my family had suffered from my work addiction, my heart and soul were in pain. I was overwhelmed and exhausted from forcing things to work in my life, yet I didn't know how to let go of the control. "Please," I cried out to God. "I've had enough. Help me to find and live my true purpose. My way just does not work!" I asked God to remove my enormous need for validation and recognition from others and seek true validation from him.

I knew I would need help to keep in step with God's work in me. I turned to three male friends. We shared our struggles with family, mar riage and work, and became soulful advocates for one another. Gone was the pretense of having the perfect life. We were simply "two or three gathered in his name" (see Matthew 18:20). We read books, studied the Bible together and spent time exploring life outside of our work worlds. In this environment I wasn't judged, nor did I judge. It was much like being cocooned in order to experience a deep, divine work of transformation.

I felt led to resign as senior pastor of the largest church in town. After a brief sabbatical, God showed me my true calling. Instead of pastoring megachurches, I now felt a God-given desire to pastor microchurches of two to three people. Free from demands of budgets and buildings, I could be a companion to a few instead of a leader of the masses. These days, our ministry facilitates retreats that invite others to experience the transformation of the Potter's hands. The Potter's Inn offers soul care to people on the fast lane who want to live with heart and save their souls from destruction. It is the confluence of our gifts, passion and experience. I no longer believe in the magic formulas to the good life that are extolled in shelves and shelves of self-help books.

In "small places" and retreats, I've learned to offer my battered heart to others and invite them to walk the path of transformation with me. The connections I longed for with others have been restored as I've stepped out of my isolation and opened myself to others.

My own family became a place where I experienced the fruit of transformation. The longing for authentic transformation required that I give up my megadreams of an illustrious career and embrace my microfamily as the starting place for the deep change I wanted and needed. I began to give my wife and sons time with me to bridge the chasm that had formed between us. We took long walks together in the woods and learned to talk to one another again. We camped in the wilderness in a pop-up trailer. A wonderful sense of aliveness seemed to flow through me. God, nature and my family restored my painful soul.

I was becoming more sensitive, more human, more alive as my heart awakened. The world acted as a sort of mentor as I witnessed God's fingerprints in those long walks. In fact, these walks have become a signature event in our own ministry. We call them "God Walks" because they introduce our busy retreat participants to the simplicity of silence and solitude that a walk through nature or a city park can provide.

My wife and I moved from functioning as ministry partners to serving as life companions for one another who love and support one another in our woundedness. It has taken time and being more intentional to guard our new learned intimacy with one another and to reclaim the ground we lost.

As of this writing, sixteen years have passed since that pivotal year for me. Now in my fifties, I'm more grateful than ever that I invited God to transform my heart.

Has my life been perfect since? Were all of my problems solved? Absolutely not! Transformation didn't mean I wouldn't suffer or experience hard times. After all, the Bible reminds us, it rains on the just and the unjust. A few years ago my wife was diagnosed with breast cancer. One year later while hiking in the Grand Canyon my youngest son almost died from a ruptured appendix. He remained in the hospital for more than a month. These experiences with the people I love most offered me challenging opportunities to truly live and be a transformed man.

THE PROCESS OF TRANSFORMATION

Transformation is *never* complete. I am no trophy of transformation, only a man in the process of transformation. I can only confess (and you can confess with me):

God uses flawed men to accomplish his purposes.

I am a flawed man.

I am a man in process.

God is using me now and will continue to use me in the future to accomplish what he desires.

I am not perfect, but I am available.

Come, O God, and transform my heart.

There is both glory and ruin in our hearts. The ruin in our hearts is easier to see. It's that mess inside of us, the residue of sin that has colored everything in life, including our hearts, to motley gray. The ruin in our hearts is of our making—the mistakes and missteps that mar us. It's the sin and guilt inside of us that has twisted, hardened and gnarled our hearts against God's design for us. The glory is harder to see: it is knowing that Christ is there and knowing that he takes up residence inside of us. The glory is seeing ourselves as objects of God's passionate creation and affection. The glory places us on the receiving end of sacred love. The glory is Jesus Christ dwelling in our hearts.

Consider the worksheet on pages 22-23. Scan the three filled columns, paying careful attention to the longing in your heart for "authentic transformation" and the stirrings of self-recognition as you read about "pseudo-transformation." Then evaluate some of your own attempts to address the ruin and to lean into the glory in your heart by filling in the fourth column.

THE JOURNEY TO OUR HIDDEN CENTER

Once we've committed to the journey toward authentic transformation as opposed to the pseudo-transformation of tips and techniques or an instant cure-all, our imaginations can help us understand the transformation process. When we envision our hearts as instruments of clay that the Potter shapes and reshapes with strong and loving hands, we relax more. We accept unpredictable circumstances and crises as catalysts for change and transformation. We envision the clay spinning on the wheel and note the different shapes and forms it takes over time. The Potter has a unique design in mind as he shapes our hidden centers into new states of being and understanding.

Many of the men you'll meet in these pages have journeyed to their hidden center. Sometimes bravely, sometimes full of fear, these men pushed on. They pressed past excuses. They surrendered to God those fears, those past events and the present turmoil that had prevented their journey within to the most amazing, remarkable and "fearfully made" sanctuary where God resides.

In most of our stories the men forged ahead with God and refused to be satisfied with anything less than authentic transformation. Some experienced the gift as a previously unexplored creative ability, a deepened marriage, a new life purpose of service and meaning, new and significant friendships or even a slowing down that matches and complements life rhythms. Some relied on prayer; others came alive through journaling their journey. All of the men found their personal and unique ways to lean toward God. In all cases their formerly hard hearts were softened— paradoxically bringing forth stronger, more resilient men.

Let's join some ordinary men as they explore their hearts and share their stories of transformation. Listen with your heart as they courageously examine what lies below the waterline.

Watch them

- make room in their hearts for Jesus
- let Jesus transform their hard-hearted natures
- become men after God's own heart
- speak from the heart
- live with heart

The real transformation of a man involves his heart. If we are to be transformed, God must have access to that sacred place within. Let the transformation begin!

Transformation Worksheet

Authentic Transformation *Important ingredients in the process and journey*	Pseudo-transformation *Where we've been before—previously explored territory*	My Story *God's fingerprints in my life.*	Your Story
Faces the truth: I want to experience authentic transformation in a specific area (Romans 7:15-25; John 8:31-32)	Perpetuates a lie and excuses behavior: • "I don't have a problem." • "Everyone does this."	I had to face the truth about my life and admit what I needed, what was missing.	
Admits brokenness: I cannot change myself. I need God's help to truly transform. It is beyond my own strength or abilities. (2 Corinthians 4:7-12)	Portrays polished façade: • "There's nothing wrong with me." • "Everyone else is doing this."	I realized what I had done when my son confronted me.	
Embraces a process: Transformation is not a quick fix. Becoming like Jesus involves time and mistakes. (Jeremiah 18:1-6; Ephesians 4:13-15; 2 Corinthians 3:18; 1 John 3:2)	Frantically looks for quick answers: • steps • logic • laws • tips • techniques	I gave up the quest for success by looking for the right book or technique.	
Requires surrender and humility: I can't do it alone. God, please help me. (Matthew 26:39; James 4:10; 1 Peter 5:6)	Insists on self-help and self-reliance. Keeps the struggle a secret.	I gave up on the power of my self-will. I relied on God's guidance.	

Transformation Worksheet, continued

Authentic Transformation *Important ingredients in the process and journey*	Pseudo-transformation *Where we've been before—previously explored territory*	My Story *God's fingerprints in my life.*	Your Story
Inside-out change: Authentic transformation requires more than changing on the surface. (Matthew 23:25; Mark 7:18-23)	Outside, external change: • preoccupied with appearances • concerned with reputation. • "What will others think of me?"	I was done with superficial self-improvement; I took a deep look at my heart with an eye toward true, DNA-level change.	
Collaborative and cooperative: I need encouragement, help and accountability to experience authentic transformation. I cannot do this by myself. (Philippians 2:12; Ecclesiastes 4:9-12; Matthew 18:19-20)	Competitive and judgmental: • desperado/Lone Ranger mentality • critical of others who seem far behind. • ungracious toward others who fail	I sought out others to accompany me on this quest. I opened myself to their feedback. Along the way I became more accepting of others, more forgiving and less judgmental.	
Personalized process: What works for you may not work for me. Trusting that God knows me and is familiar with all my ways means that God knows what I need for change. (Psalm 139:13-15)	Cookie-cutter: • "If I could find the right program or method, I'd really change." • "I'll wait till the next book or program comes out."	I recognized that what seemed to be working for others may not work for me. I committed to a personal process.	

2

THE SPIRITUAL JOURNEY

EMBRACING TRANSFORMATION

Howard Baker

As I reached the trailhead, my watch displayed 5:30 on a clear, crisp Colorado morning. I had planned the night before to get an early start in order to watch the sun rise over the Rocky Mountains. Somehow I hoped the clarity and brightness of the morning would burn away the hazy fog that had clouded my mind and heart. But just the reverse occurred. Shortly after beginning the trek up Monte Cristo Gulch I found myself scrambling over rocks and through brush with no trail in sight. My internal confusion was now externally visible. The invigorating morning hike I had imagined devolved into frustration and weariness.

When I had given up hope of finding the trail and was about to turn back, there it was! A short, steep climb placed me back on the marked path for the remainder of the ascent. Though still strenuous, the hike now had a completely different feel. I was motivated and energized. The beauty of the mountain dawn, hidden by earlier frustration, now captivated me. This is what I had hoped for!

What was it that transformed my trip up the mountain from weary wandering into joyful journey? The *awareness* that I was on the path changed everything. Secure in the knowledge that I was headed somewhere, I was set free to enjoy the journey.

Let me say it up front as clearly as I can: We are on a journey; this journey is what life is about; this journey is *all* that life is about. That is the reality. But awareness of the journey is another matter, and a decisive one at that. Not knowing the path creates the weary frustration that leads men to give up the journey entirely, just as I was about to give up my morning hike. Knowing the path gives a comprehensive and transforming vision for life that is described by the apostle Paul, "For me, to live is Christ and to die is gain" (Philippians 1:21). Indeed, it's everything we have hoped for!

THE JOURNEY METAPHOR

How then do we become so aware of the path we are called to that our lives are transformed as a result? The biblical and classical image of "journey" provides a robust metaphor to frame this life of following Jesus and to order our imaginations. It captures the attributes of movement, purpose and destination that comprise the process of Christ being formed in us. If this is a new concept to you, it may be helpful to think in terms of the relationship of a wedding to marriage. The wedding is not the goal. It is the beginning. I couldn't wait to grab my new bride, leave that reception and begin our life together. In the same way, trusting Christ is not an arrival but the starting point of an eternal journey of union and communion that begins here and now.

The journey image especially helps us as we move through the changing seasons of life. When we experience doubt, apathy, disillusionment or depression, our first reaction is, *What did I do wrong?* The fact that my spiritual development is a journey explains these conditions as normal passages that we, as men, move through. They are more often "providential permissions" rather than personal failures. Think of the many examples of biblical heroes who were placed in positions of hardship by God and emerged from them as transformed men: Moses in the Midian wilderness, Joseph in the Egyptian prison, David hiding in caves, Daniel in the lions' den, Jonah in the belly of a fish, Job in the pit of despair, Jeremiah beaten and in stocks, Jesus on the cross. Can you think of your current situation in this light? Is it possible that what you are experiencing at this very moment is part of a journey that is being guided by your loving Father? Could it be that God is as interested in developing your faith as he was in developing Moses', Joseph's and all the rest?

The story of Sarapion, a desert father of fourth-century Egypt, illustrates how we are each on an individual journey. On a pilgrimage to Rome, Sarapion heard of a celebrated recluse, a woman who never left her small room. As an incessant wanderer Sarapion was skeptical of her way of life. He visited her and asked, "Why are you sitting here?" To which she replied, "I am not sitting. I am on a journey."[1] Whether wanderers or sitters, it is helpful for us to realize that growing in Christ is a journey with many surprising twists and turns rather than a linear progression that can be controlled and predicted. It's a roller coaster, not a merry-go-round. Just when I begin to think that by virtue of my decisions, strategies and action plans I am in charge of my own growth, the bottom drops out. It may be a huge disappointment at work, a conflict with my wife or something more personal, such as creeping doubts in my own faith. Whatever the disturbance, the message is clear: I am not in control. While part of me wants to fight to regain control, my truer self enjoys the freedom of letting God be in charge. The scriptural and historical reality is that we move on in the spiritual journey when God wants us to, for God causes the growth (1 Corinthians 3:6). I, for one, am glad it's not up to me.

THE JOURNEY OF JESUS

This journey metaphor is woven throughout Israel's history, and God led the people he called on many journeys. Abraham's journey began "even though he did not know where he was going" (Hebrews 11:8), which is often true with the obedient believer. We don't always know where God is taking us, but by faith we move out, as Abraham did. Moses' journey took him from Egypt to Midian and back to Egypt to deliver his people. It continued with forty years of wandering in the wilderness. The journey continued for God's people as they moved in and took possession of the Promised Land. The Psalms of Ascents (Psalms 120—134) were journey songs sung by the faithful as they traveled up to Jerusalem on their pilgrimage to worship at the temple three times a year. Then there was the traumatic evacuation into exile in Babylon. All of these experiences etched the journey image into the collective memory of Israel.

Jesus gathered up the history of the nation's journey of faith by proclaiming, "I am the way" (John 14:6). The Greek word for "way" is *odos,* from which we get our words *odometer* and *exodus.* Just as the exodus was God's decisive saving act for Israel, so Jesus is our "exodus," our journey out of sin and bondage to new life in the promised land of the kingdom of God. All four Gospels use the journey motif in narrating the life of Jesus, but according to Richard Byrne,

> Luke's Gospel sets the public ministry of Jesus largely within the context of one great journey from Galilee to Jerusalem (Lk 9:51-19:27). "When the days for his being taken up were fulfilled, Jesus resolutely determined to journey to Jerusalem" (Lk 9:51). Jesus chooses a course from which he will not divert. Luke intended to present Jesus as a model for the spiritual journey of every human being from the Galilee of self-discovery and self-awareness to the Jerusalem of self-sacrifice before God. For the heart of Jerusalem was the temple, and the heart of the temple was the altar of sacrifice. To understand the message of Jesus, according to Luke, is to make this journey with him.[2]

This was such a new thought for me: Luke presents Jesus as a model of the spiritual journey for every man. If I call myself his follower, then I follow him into "self-discovery and self-awareness" that can be as exhilarating for us as feeding the five thousand was for Jesus. If I stay on the journey, it will eventually lead to my personal Jerusalem of surrender and sacrifice.

Indeed, Jesus calls each of us to the challenging journey of denying ourselves, taking up the cross and following him. In the Sermon on the Mount this journey is referred to as the "narrow . . . road that leads to life" (Matthew 7:14). The early disciples responded to this call of Jesus and were called people of the Way before they were called Christians (Acts 11:26).[3] Both individually and as members of Christ's body, the church, we are people of the Way, people on the journey with Christ. This defines who I am and what my life is about. It's not about success, status, acquisitions or happiness. It is about staying faithful to the Way until I reach the destination for which I am making this journey and to which I am called by God.

THE JOURNEY'S END

"Begin with the end in mind" is more important as a proverb for the spiritual journey than for project management. Having a clear picture of my destination allows me to make sense of my journey, even when I feel I am going in the opposite direction to what I had planned. Times of dryness or darkness are always difficult and challenging, but if I understand how they help me arrive at my ultimate destination I can welcome them as normal and necessary parts of my journey with Christ. Or as Bernard of Clairvaux put it in the twelfth century, "when you have heard what the reward is, the labor of the climb will be less."[4]

So what is that reward? Is it the good life or "being blessed" or going to heaven or a life of purpose and significance? While these may be part of our experience as followers of Jesus, they are also examples of inadequate and less than biblical notions of the journey's end.

The true goal of the journey is captured succinctly by the apostle John, "Dear friends, now we are children of God, and what we will be has not yet been made known. But we know that when he appears, we shall be like him, for we shall see him as he is" (1 John 3:2).

Seeing Jesus face to face and becoming like him are the two dimensions of our destination—communion and union. Unlike a physical journey in which you are either at your destination or not, the goal of the spiritual journey is progressively realized. As I walk with Christ, my communion with him deepens and matures. The simultaneous result of greater intimacy is growth in Christlikeness. Likeness is the result of communion. I become like Jesus by being with him. Living my life with him transforms me from the inside out.

According to Romans 8:28-29, God is working all things together to conform me to the image of his Son. These verses are often used in an attempt to comfort those in painful circumstances by pointing out the truth that God will work everything out for the "good." Whether this actually comforts those suffering is another discussion. What needs to be taken seriously is that the "good" that Paul refers to in this passage is God's purpose of conforming us to the image of Christ. Therefore, when I am clear about the destination of my journey, I can view every circumstance as an opportunity for spiritual formation in Christ. There is nothing that is outside the reach of God's redemptive hand. The courageous young Christian with cerebral palsy embodies the intent of these verses by saying, "I would rather have cerebral palsy and know Christ than to be in perfect health and not know him." This is the perspective that distinguishes the spiritual pilgrim from the spiritual tourist. Tourists go wherever mood, pleasure or whim takes them. Pilgrims always have one eye on their destination, which gives meaning, hope and joy to their present place in the journey.

STAGES IN THE JOURNEY

"At the LORD's command Moses recorded the stages in their journey. This is their journey by stages" (Numbers 33:2). The verses that follow this verse list forty places that God instructed Moses to record. This tells me that God cares about our journeys, that there are stages in the journey and that these stages are to be noticed and recorded. In their book *The*

Critical Journey,[5] Janet Hagberg and Robert Guelich notice and record six stages of the spiritual journey that are common among Christians today:

- The Recognition of God

- The Life of Discipleship

- The Productive Life

- The Journey Inward

- The Journey Outward

- The Life of Love

Another uniquely male pattern is provided by Richard Rohr in his book *The Wild Man's Journey.* His treatment recalls the pattern of Jesus moving from self-discovery to self-sacrifice. Rohr uses the language of "ascent" and "descent." In between these movements is a "crisis of limitation."

These patterns fit my experience well. As I weave my journey into these developmental stages, I hope you become more aware of some of the significant places in your story.

THE ASCENT

Recognition. As a child I attended a small-town church where I developed an image of God as Rulegiver, Judge and Scorekeeper. This understanding prevailed until my fifth grade year when my dad contracted a life-threatening cancer of the jaw and mouth. He survived through drastic surgery that removed the right side of his jaw and most of his tongue. This experience produced in me an image of God that was personal and caring, and who answered prayer. So began the first stage of my spiritual journey—the recognition of God. It came through a powerful felt need. As I mention the various stages I went through, you may want to make some notes about how you have lived through these stages. When did you first recognize the presence of God in your life?

How did that happen? How would you describe your early image of God? When did you move from recognition to commitment and faith? How did that transpire?

Discipleship. The recognition of God is the foundation for all the stages that follow. The authors call my next stage "discipleship." The focus of my four years in college and an additional four years in seminary was on learning about God through the Scriptures. Truth was paramount. Every question required an answer. Every problem could be solved. Being "right" was important and there was an "us versus them" attitude between those of us who had the truth and those who didn't. During this stage, believers tend to find answers in a leader, a group or a belief system. We feel a sense of confidence and security in our faith. The core of faith at this time is knowing the truth.

Production. After graduating from seminary I was anxious to put into practice all the knowledge I had accumulated and to do "great things for God." While preserving some time for family life I gave the rest of my energy to ministry. My efforts were well intentioned but misguided. I operated on the basis that God would bless hard work, so the effectiveness of my ministry was very much up to me. For many men this stage of "production" is a time of discovering and implementing their calling and gifts. They often find a place of service in the church and success in the marketplace. Careers are built, financial security is acquired and families are established. It all looks very impressive.

These first three stages are for a man what Rohr calls the "ascent." Here are some sound-bite descriptors for this period in a man's life: "more is more," "ego-driven solo journey," "first half of life," "fulfilling dreams," "reaching goals," "experience of personal power and influence," "climbing the ladder," "tyranny of the urgent," "life is a game to win," "what you do overshadows who you are," "in control." The ruling passion in a man during the ascent could be accomplishment, accumulation, power or significance, or some combination of those. For me the ascent was all about ministry accomplishment and success under the guise of serving God. But I grew weary in doing well and life became a performance.

Let me point out that the journey of ascent is both natural and necessary for a man's development. We read in Luke 2:52 that Jesus experienced physical, mental, social and spiritual growth as a young man, just as any healthy man does. The ascent can be navigated in a life-giving and redemptive manner, as Jesus did. But many men, and I am a prime example, get caught in the web of ego, ambition and self-importance—until confronted rather suddenly with a crisis.

A Crisis of Limitation: The Inward Journey

In the famous words of Dante's *Inferno,* I had come to the middle of life and "I found myself astray in a dark wood." Success no longer seemed to satisfy. Failure created deep disillusionment. I was forced to look inward. There was a gnawing emptiness that refused to be filled by what had always worked before. For two years everything I tried had the rotten smell of yesterday's manna. Other phrases that describe this stage in the journey include: "loss of meaning," "pain of failure," "significant losses," "search for significance," "pain transformed or transmitted," "midlife issues," "beginning to let go."

This inner focus is normally precipitated by some sort of crisis. It could be external, such as the loss of a job or a marriage, or it could be the internal loss of faith, purpose or meaning. In either case, it is a crisis of limitation. The old resources that I had depended on no longer worked. This can be a dark and painful phase of the journey, punctuated with losses. John of the Cross described an intense version of this stage as a "dark night of the soul." Few of us will be led into those depths, but at some point we all will be led by the Spirit to turn inward and rediscover the love and power of the indwelling Christ.

For me this crisis lasted for a couple of years. The light began to break through while on a four-day silent retreat. My whole life was turned upside down as the result of experiencing the reality of Jesus and his unchanging love for me. My new passion was intimacy with God rather than service for him. I surrendered my ego need for success and significance. It was like a second conversion.

DESCENDING WITH JESUS: THE OUTWARD JOURNEY

The inner journey leads us into the process of discovering more of our true selves. We realize that we have a good deal of inner work to do in order to find our true self in Christ. This can take a significant amount of time. Eventually we are ready to journey outward from a new and deeper foundation in Christ. For me this involved a change of location and a change of vocation. The outer journey can look very similar to the life of production, but the energy and motivation are completely different. I am no longer striving to accomplish great things for God, but I am learning to surrender to God's ways and purposes. The journey outward proceeds from a sense of living out of the deep center of God's presence. It is a descent. It is downward mobility. It is the way of the Suffering Servant, the way of the cross.

A person in this stage experiences deep peace; he takes delight in simply being God's man and is able to see God in all aspects of life. Such a man seems to be careless about what many consider the important things because he has completely surrendered his future, his family, his finances, his status and his significance to God. For example, one close friend of mine stepped down from a privileged role as a world-traveling executive of a major corporation in order to be at home with his family. There was a huge financial sacrifice involved. In a culture of unceasing ascent my friend looks like a fool, but in the kingdom of God he may be among the greatest.

THE LIFE OF LOVE

The final stage, the life of love, is expressed by the apostle Paul when he says that for him "to live is Christ and to die is gain" (Philippians 1:21). Many may have momentary experiences of this kind of life, but there are precious few who are willing to die so completely to self that their life becomes Christ. It is difficult to describe these men. They are simply vessels that have been filled by the Spirit and overflow to everyone around them. Out of their deep and authentic selves flow rivers of living water. Almost naturally they lay down their lives for their friends, following the example of Jesus in living the life of love.

God is directing each of our journeys. We need not fret over where we find ourselves at the present. What we must guard against is resisting or quenching the Holy Spirit when the Spirit is drawing us to a new phase of life. We are called to be clay in the Potter's hands, soft and pliable. All we need to concern ourselves with is yielding to God's gentle or disruptive movements in our lives and the Lord will take responsibility for our progress on the journey.

TRAIL MARKERS OF TRANSFORMATION

Though by no means are these movements universal, they do seem to be common to men who are faithfully following the Lord. As the Spirit of God draws us along the journey of life there are several directional movements, trailmarkers of transformation, that we can notice and cooperate with. God is moving us from

- action to prayer
- control to surrender
- working for God to letting God work through me
- many false selves to the one true self in Christ
- external righteousness to faith, hope, love
- initiating to responding
- individualism to community
- personal goals to communion with God
- self-sufficiency to poverty of spirit

If you sense yourself moving in these directions, you can be confident that you are cooperating with God's work in your soul, that transformation is happening and that you are headed toward your journey's destination of communion and union with Christ.

THE SPIRITUAL DISCIPLINES: THE UNFORCED RHYTHMS OF GRACE FOR THE JOURNEY

We cooperate with God's sovereign work of transformation through the spiritual disciplines. Tragically the true intent and practice of the disciplines have been co-opted by our activist, self-help culture. This explains how the promised life of rest looks more like anxious striving and how the simple coming to Jesus and learning from him have been made to appear complicated and out of reach for the ordinary disciple.

Ways of receiving. First and foremost, spiritual disciplines are "means of grace"—ways of receiving something from God, not doing something for him. They work on us, not on God. They are ways of accessing the infinite resources of the kingdom of God for our lives. If you have an ATM card you understand how this works. You could have thousands of dollars in your bank account, but if you don't have a card and a PIN number you don't have access to what is rightfully yours. The spiritual disciplines provide access to the abundant life—the kingdom within that Jesus has given us. When Jesus spent forty days fasting in solitude in the desert before facing the tempter, he was receiving strength for the battle ahead—accessing resources from the Father. So we follow Jesus into his practices to gain, as he did, the power to face the challenges and trials of life.

Brownies not broccoli. I eat my broccoli because it's good for me (and my wife makes me). I eat a brownie because it's *good!* So when you think of the spiritual disciplines are you thinking broccoli or brownies? Once we make the connection that an intentional life of following Jesus is not just "good for us" but really good, the best life possible, we have "brownie" motivation. The disciplines are warm, rich brownies for the soul—much tastier than chicken soup! How might it change your approach to life if your thought was "I *get to* practice the spiritual disciplines," instead of "I *have to* practice the disciplines"?

Disciplines not discipline. Jesus described the life of following him as the "easy" yoke in Matthew 11:28-30. There is a dual word picture here. The immediate one is that of a stronger, older ox yoked with a smaller, younger one. All that is left to the smaller ox in order not to feel the weight of the load is to walk in step alongside his more competent partner. So for us, the disciplines are ways to help us keep in step with Jesus, casting our cares on him, so that he is pulling the weight of life for us. They keep our lives in rhythm with Jesus'. Living this way is the easy yoke—far easier and lighter than carrying the burdens of life myself.

The other more subtle word picture comes from the world of the Jewish rabbi whose set of interpretations of the *Torah,* God's loving instruction to his people, was called his "yoke." These rabbis had elaborate and detailed prescriptions of how to live according to *Torah* that required strict discipline. Jesus comes along and proclaims that his yoke is easy because he reduces the hundreds of complex commandments of the other rabbis to the simplicity of loving God and loving neighbor. It is also easy because, as he teaches in the Sermon on the Mount, obedience flows from the inside out. The inner transformation produced by the spiritual disciplines frees me to inwardly become the kind of person who loves God and others outwardly. As Dallas Willard has said, the disciplines "enable me to do what I cannot do by direct effort."[6]

For example, I can't by a decision of my will simply decide to love my irritating coworker at the office when my heart is filled with anger toward him or her. However, by using the spiritual discipline of praying the psalms I can learn to pray my anger as the psalmists do, freeing me to love those who previously angered me. Rather than trying harder through discipline to be more patient with my children, I can enter into the spiritual discipline of silence for ten minutes a day and allow the inner peace created to flow into my family relationships.

A LIFE THAT IS UNFORCED

Immediately after young David had accepted the challenge to fight Goliath, Saul forced his armor on David, thinking what had worked for him as king would work for David (1 Samuel 17:38-39). It didn't. David could barely walk with the ill-fitting armor, so he discarded it for what was congenial to his experience, strengths and current situation—five smooth stones and a slingshot. These tools of David would have been of no use to Saul or the other soldiers, just as their armor was of no use to David. Forcing someone else's armor on myself doesn't work in military battle, nor does it work in spiritual battle. Yet many followers of Christ seem to be trying to wear their pastor's armor or armor from a book they have read or the armor of a ministry they have served. As a result, like David, they can hardly walk, stumbling in the life of faith.

It is about you! Contrary to what I may initially and unselfishly think, my relationship with Jesus has to be tailored to the unique creation of God that I am and the unique journey that I am on. If the infinite Creator God has chosen to create each human as his workmanship, literally his "poem" (Greek, *poiema,* Ephesians 2:10), don't you think his ongoing work of creating and saving individuals will be beautifully and individually crafted? This means that each man's response to his creating and saving God is original and creative work. It is creative in the sense that he is responding to God out of the materials of *his* life, just as an artist creates using paints, musical notes or words. Cooperating with my Creator and Redeemer, I become the artist of my own life.

Francis de Sales, some five hundred years ago, reflected an ancient wisdom that surpasses our own when he wrote, "Devotion must be exercised in different ways by the gentleman, the worker, the servant, the prince, the widow, the young girl, and the married woman. Not only is this true, but the practice of devotion must also be adapted to the strength, activities, and duties of each particular person."[7] This is the freedom for which Christ has set us free (Galatians 5:1), to develop a personal and intimate relationship with God in the real and ordinary circumstances of my life. This is not out of reach for any of us.

Pray as you can, not as you can't. This sounds obvious but it is surprising how often sincere pray-ers impose on themselves ways of praying that are as ill-fitting as Saul's armor was for David. Rather than hand-me-down prayers, we have been given a custom-tailored wardrobe of conversation with God. As André Louf puts it,

> Authentic prayer can never be learnt from someone else. It has its own instructor within it. Prayer is God's gift to the man who prays. . . . Thus prayer is the precious fruit of the Word—Word of God that has become wholly our own and in that way has been inscribed deep in our body and our psyche, and that now can become our response to the love of the Father. The Spirit stammers it out in our heart, without our doing anything about it. It bubbles up, it flows, it runs like living water.[8]

When you are struggling with prayer, you might try an assignment that many have found helpful: for as long as you can, don't pray, but when you realize that you can't *not* pray, what sort of prayer arises within you? What "bubbles up" is the kind of prayer that is most "you." Start there, be attentive to the unique gift of prayer given you, and pray as you can.

A LIFE THAT IS IN RHYTHM

My first encounter with the world of spiritual disciplines was over twenty years ago when I first read Richard Foster's wonderful book *The Celebration of Discipline*. I loved it, but I saw little hope of integrating what I had read into an already full life of a young family and demanding job. It seemed to be an all-or-nothing proposition—a disciplined life with Christ or the conventional life of hurry and flurry. What escaped me was the possibility of a *via media,* a middle way between the two opposites. The middle way is learning from Jesus how to live into God's rhythms of work and sabbath, feasting and fasting, community and solitude, service and study, interaction and silence.

Learn from Jesus. To be a disciple is to be a student or apprentice of a master. Jesus is the Master of life, the expert on the kind of life that glo-

rifies the Father, serves others and provides the ultimate personal fulfillment. Here are some suggestions for learning from Jesus how to live in
his kingdom through the practice of the spiritual disciplines.

1. Take seriously your situation in life and choose a few disciplines accordingly. The commuter could use drive time as a sanctuary on
   wheels to worship, listen or be still before the Lord.

2. When do you profoundly experience God's presence? Be intentional
   about committing to your spiritual disciplines around that place or
   event. If it is through the beauty of God's creation, then plan to take
   a walk with Jesus on an outdoor trail twice a week.

3. Don't be afraid to experiment with a variety of practices. Incorpo-
   rate those that are helpful and discard the ones that aren't. For example, it is easy to get in a rut with Bible reading. One year read
   through the entire Bible, but the next *slowly* read and meditate
   through one book monthly.

4. Add and delete disciplines as needed as your journey progresses.
   There are seasons and rhythms to pay attention to in this creative relationship with the God who loves us. The father of young children
   may not have the option of enjoying extended times of solitude, but
   he can practice the presence of God (See Brother Lawrence's *The Practice of the Presence of God*) in the midst of taking the kids to the park
   or mowing the lawn.

The magnetic attraction of holiness. As I follow Jesus into his practices
of communion with the Father, my life begins to have that same powerful attraction that his did. In a world of anger and hate, a life of love stops
folks in their tracks. For the anxious and restless, a life filled with the
peace of God is irresistible. This is why the multitudes were drawn to
Jesus. This is why thousands went to the wilderness to find the desert
father Anthony in the fourth century. Centuries later it is why journal-
ists, TV cameras, indeed, the whole world beat a path to the door of a
diminutive Albanian nun in Calcutta: Mother Teresa. And this is why

you, right where you are, can be, as Jesus said, "the light of the world" and "the salt of the earth" (Matthew 5:13-14) simply by living "the unforced rhythms of grace" (Matthew 11:29 *The Message*).

As I progress on the spiritual journey, there is a quiet transformation that occurs in my life. God seems to change, but in reality I am the one who has changed. This is beautifully illustrated in the exchange between Aslan, the lion Christ figure, and the young girl Lucy from C. S. Lewis's Chronicles of Narnia:

> "Welcome, child," he said.
> "Aslan," said Lucy, "you're bigger."
> "That is because you are older, little one," answered he.
> "Not because you are?"
> "I am not. But every year you grow, you will find me bigger."[9]

As we grow in our love for, experience of and obedience to Christ, he looms larger and larger so that we can begin to say with the apostle Paul, "For to me, to live is Christ" (Philippians 1:21). And we gladly join John the Baptist in proclaiming, "He must increase, but I must decrease" (John 3:30 KJV).

PART ONE

INWARD

3

INTIMACY WITH GOD

GROWING THROUGH THE YEARS

Doug Stewart

Since my youth, O God, you have taught me,
and to this day I declare your marvelous deeds.
Even when I am old and gray,
do not forsake me, O God,
till I declare your power to the next generation,
your might to all who are to come.

PSALM 71:17-18

Often our lives can only be understood in retrospect. Jacob, patriarch of the twelve tribes of Israel, said toward the end of his life, "God . . . has been my shepherd all my life to this day" (Genesis 48:15). Certainly for most of his life he didn't feel he had a shepherd; rather, he thought everything depended on him and his wits. But God's persistent care and gracious interventions finally brought him to see that in reality *God had been there all along, drawing him closer.*

God loves us, as Scripture and God's people declare without ceasing, and he desires good things for us. Divine love, the true love behind all that is, is outgoing and seeks to create relationships. God will go to any length, overcome all resistance, find a way through all obstacles and pay every price to bring us into intimacy with himself. No price is too great for him to pay, as Paul declares: "He who did not spare his own Son, but gave him up for us all—how will he not also, along with him, graciously give us all things?" (Romans 8:32).

God wants us to be intimate with him, like a parent with child, a husband with wife or a friend with friend. We know this because Scripture uses these images. We also know it because of Jesus: "the only Son, who is close to the Father's heart, who has made him known" (John 1:18 NRSV). Through Jesus God reveals that he loves us passionately and longs for an intimate relationship with us. Jesus' disciples called him "Lord and Teacher." They saw themselves as his servants; yet he called them "friends" (John 15:14-15). He told them, "As the Father has loved me, so have I loved you," and he invited them to "remain in my love" (John 15:9). In *The Message,* Eugene Peterson translates this as "I've loved you the way my Father has loved me. Make yourselves at home in my love."

Jesus wants us to enjoy and share the same kind of relationship with him that he has with the Father. The Father loves the Son above all things (Matthew 17:5; John 3:35), and the Son loves the Father in the same way (John 14:31). Jesus promises similar intimacy with us: "You will realize that I am in my Father, and you are in me, and I am in you" (John 14:20). He said, "If anyone loves me . . . my Father will love him, and we will come to him and make our home with him" (John 14:23). He wants to live with us now, and for us to live with him forever!

Nothing is better than knowing the infinitely powerful and wise—but gentle and tender—God, who made us for himself, and whose Son gave himself for us (Galatians 2:20). But intimacy with God requires that we too want it. We must be willing to risk a relationship with him. Knowing him depends on our becoming like him. His love is holy and pure; it has no darkness in it, and he doesn't allow darkness to remain in us (1 John 1:6). The apostle Paul says that becoming like him involves "sharing in his sufferings" (Philippians 3:10).

The apostles John, Peter and Paul are examples of the transformation God offers. In Scripture we are shown their weaknesses and dark sides, but their changed lives give glory to God.

John was one of the "Sons of Thunder." He wanted Jesus to wipe out the Samaritans when they refused hospitality. John revealed his partisan spirit when he tried to stop exorcists who acted in Jesus' name but who weren't Jesus' disciples. He, along with his brother James, sought places of honor in the coming kingdom of God. Yet John became known as the apostle of love.

Peter resisted Jesus' announcements of his future rejection and suffering. He protested at Jesus' washing his feet and later fled from the path of suffering for Jesus, even denying any association with him. Yet Jesus called on him to shepherd the church and build on the foundation he laid.

Paul was hard-driving, competitive, intolerant and hard-hearted, yet he could ultimately testify to a wholly different life direction because of the love of Christ:

> I want to know Christ and the power of his resurrection and the fellowship of sharing in his sufferings, becoming like him in his death, and so, somehow, to attain to the resurrection from the dead.
>
> Not that I have already obtained all this, or have already been made perfect, but I press on to take hold of that for which Christ Jesus took hold of me. (Philippians 3:10-12)

The experience of change and transformation I see in John, Paul and Peter gives me much hope. God's surpassing love had transformed them.

MY OWN JOURNEY TOWARD INTIMACY WITH GOD

I am who I am because of the good Shepherd's loving pursuit of me. I would like to say that I have sought and welcomed the changes he has led me to; the truth is, I have resisted them much of the time. Thus whatever transformation I have experienced has taken place because I have encountered the loving God. Along the way God has had to overcome my fear of him, my desire to keep him at a distance and my resistance to letting his love into my life.

As a young child I was the delight of my parents and the focus of their love. They continually let me know I was loved, and I found security and joy in it. Their love marked me and moved me to seek similar love from others.

During my teenage years, my father was overtaken by a prolonged depression and effectively dropped out of my life. He became very fragile, and our family had to protect him and learn to function without him in many ways. For a young man who looked up to and wanted his father's affirmation and approval, this loss was deeply felt. It left me without a model and anchor. I felt restless, longing for meaning and significance—and love. It seemed I was on my own to make something out of my life. While this restlessness and inner drivenness pushed me to do well in sports, social life and academics, it also led to trouble: I sought excitement. I suffered painful consequences from bad choices—and from getting caught! I became despondent about what had happened and fearful about what more might happen to me. I could no longer trust that I really could do well on my own. I was lonely and looking for a better way.

At this low point in my life I heard that some in my school were having remarkable experiences with Christ, life-changing experiences that they readily talked about. (I am from Charlotte, North Carolina, part of the Bible Belt. Everyone I knew went to church, as I always had, and was a "Christian," but no one had ever spoken to me about a personal relationship with Christ.) When a girlfriend invited me to a church retreat, I decided I was ready to give it a try. I had no idea what I was getting into, but I knew I needed something. At the end of the retreat when the call to accept Christ was given, I stood to acknowledge that I was "accepting Jesus Christ as my personal Lord and Savior." Night changed to day, sadness to joy, fear to peace, emptiness to overflow. I had never experienced anything like what (who) was coming into my life.

This was over fifty years ago. In retrospect, I realize that God gave me a taste of his love, a love for which I had been made and shaped, and the experience of that love created in me a thirst for more. I got hooked after the first experience! Subsequent experiences have only deepened my thirst and longing, both through the pain felt by the absence of his love when I've run from him and by times of finding ever greater delight in knowing more of the love of Christ "that surpasses knowledge" (Ephesians 3:19).

One of the unpleasant byproducts of coming to know Christ and determining to follow him wholeheartedly was that I lost some good friends. My friends who still pursued my old lifestyle drew away from me. Naturally, many thought I'd "become religious" and gone off the deep end. (Perhaps I had, but I sure did like the water I was in!)

The following year I went to college, determined to follow Christ and make him known to others. Again, I found myself very much alone and threatened by the options before me. My college was an elite school that attracted those who had the personal ambition to succeed and talents to match it. I was feeling lonely and wondered if I was making bad choices. Doubts assaulted me and self-pity came to visit. Yet in my loneliness and struggle, God met my deepest needs. I learned, probably out of desperation and a hungering heart, to seek him in my loneliness. I knew that he had taken hold of me, and I couldn't walk away from him.

Perhaps the deepest lesson that came from those years is that God can be known personally, and knowing him is the highest delight that life offers. In my subsequent years of ministry I continued to draw from the well of his love. (I have since realized that in God's providence he called me to "pioneering" ministry that involved a lot of time alone; I needed to know how to drink deeply from the well of living water—his continual presence.) God was schooling me in the spiritual disciplines of solitude and silence, teaching me to be with "God alone" (Psalm 62:1). Being alone with God is still for me the primary way of tasting anew of his love and grace, and hearing his words of encouragement, correction, guidance and affirmation.

CHANNELS OF GOD'S LOVE

One way in particular that God has drawn me into his love is through the Scriptures. In my early years as a Christian and later in InterVarsity Christian Fellowship, I was taught to honor and love the Scriptures, to submit to them, to learn from them, and most of all to seek to know God through them. As I was led to pastoral ministry about twenty years ago, I returned again and again to the Scriptures to increase my understanding of what pastoral ministry was about. Through prayerful reading, searching, studying and meditating on the Bible's revelation of God, insight came with growing clarity, and conviction developed with increasing strength. From beginning to end God is filling us with the knowledge of Christ's love. In the face of our deep rebellion and bondage, Paul says in Ephesians, "Because of his great love for us, God, who is rich in mercy, made us alive with Christ even when we were dead in transgressions" (Ephesians 2:4-5). He goes on:

> For this reason I kneel before the Father, from whom his whole family in heaven and on earth derives its name. I pray that out of his glorious riches he may strengthen you with power through his Spirit in your inner being, so that Christ may dwell in your hearts through faith. And I pray that you, being rooted and established in love, may have power, together with all the saints, to grasp how wide and long and high and deep is the love of Christ, and to know this love that surpasses knowledge—that you may be filled to the measure of all the fullness of God. (Ephesians 3:14-19)

That prayer captivated and convinced me that God desires to share all of himself with us in love—to be intimate with us beyond what we could ask or imagine. The Scriptures become his living words to interact directly in love with our life and needs.

Twenty years ago I spent a month with a few others in a retreat setting in an isolated village on a remote mountaintop in Switzerland. Spiritual mentor Hans Bürki introduced me to the spiritual disciplines of meditation and of lectio divina, a way of reading and listening to the Scriptures from the heart, allowing God to choose how he wanted to speak to me. What resulted were very intimate and profound encounters with God. His words addressed the deep questions, fears, desires and hopes of my heart in a way that I hadn't really known before. Prior to this, even if I had known them and been able to name these issues, I would have tried to push them aside, deny them or overcome them by willpower or by directing my attention to a spiritual enterprise. But now I was paying attention to myself and what I was experiencing—acceptable and unacceptable, pleasant and unpleasant—and allowing God through his Word and by his Spirit to speak to the real me that he knew and loved.

Simply put, allowing God to speak to me in this way revealed that he truly knew me, welcomed me with my sinful and ugly parts, cared for me and sought only good for me. This experience gave me a renewed, clearer passion to know God's love and to focus my ministry on bringing others to know the love of Christ in a greater way. The years since have been marked by ongoing intimacy with God. As I open up to him and his words in the Scriptures, he continues to meet me in my daily life. As with the disciples on the way to Emmaus, Jesus still draws near and brings living words to me through the Scriptures.

Paul says, "God has poured out his love into our hearts by the Holy Spirit, whom he has given us" (Romans 5:5). Every experience of God's love has come through the Holy Spirit's actions. Often he has used Scripture or the witness of other people, but at times the Holy Spirit simply comes, making me deeply aware that God is with me, loves me, cares for me and delights in me. He gives a profound sense of well-being, joy, peace and assurance. My cup overflows, and all I can do is receive this gift, savor it, stand still and give thanks to the One who loves me and gave himself for me. I think that God likes to surprise us with unexpected visits, just to remind us that he is always with us and delighting in us, and that his presence isn't the result of our initiatives. He just shows up because he wants to; he wants to bless us with his loving presence.

BARRIERS TO LOVE AND INTIMACY

While I can sing and celebrate the delights of God's love, I also must acknowledge that at times I resist it; I long for it but also flee from it. This unsettling paradox hasn't been easy to see and is even harder to admit. God's love is like a bright light that reveals what is ugly, defaced, dirty or hidden in me. It brings truth to my understanding and conscience that I can't hide from or explain away. My bad choices in word and deed, shameful thoughts and self-serving motivations are seen as uglier and more reproachful in the light of God's love and goodness. His purity reveals my impurity, his love my self-centeredness, his goodness my badness.

Allowing God to draw near in love means facing up to things about myself I don't like or want to see. As John says, "This is the message we have heard from him and declare to you: God is light; in him there is no darkness at all. If we claim to have fellowship with him yet walk in the darkness, we lie and do not live by the truth" (1 John 1:5-6). Intimacy with God requires honesty with him and myself. The truth of his love that draws, frees and uplifts me is also the truth of my own fear, shame and bondage, from which I need his deliverance.

God's love is even more threatening when I understand that he intends to transform me into a man who loves like he loves. Jesus' second "great" commandment, to "love your neighbor as yourself" (Matthew 22:39), sets me on a path I often resist. When he says, "Love your enemies, do good to those who hate you, bless those who curse you, pray for those who mistreat you" (Luke 6:27-28), he sets the bar impossibly high, and even worse, he forces me to admit that I don't want to do this. I not only fail embarrassingly but often don't want to do his new commandment: "Love one another. As I have loved you, so you must love one another" (John 13:34). Who can love like this?

Paradoxically, I've found that my very resistance to God's love, this fear of it and struggle against its transformational intentions, sets me up to understand and experience his love in its deepest and greatest dimension: God continues to love me, meet me, draw me to himself, removing my feelings of shame, my desires to hide or run and my painful protests about my unworthiness. Sometimes my greatest encounters with his love have come after my worst failures. Rather than scold, reproach or remind me of what I did wrong, he throws his arms around me, like the father who welcomes his prodigal son home. At other times, when I stand off from him in anger, protest and resentment, he gently pleads with me to return to his party, for I remain his beloved son.

Thankfully, I have found in these repeated experiences that God's love is enduring, persistent and unconditional. I can no more lose it than I can leave the universe. Wherever he is present, he is present in love and care, to bless and do good. The way God deals with our ingrained "evil" resistance is to "overcome evil with good" (Roman 12:21). He conquers us with his love and even turns our resistance and rejection, rebellion and sinful choices, into occasions to love us and make us into "more than conquerors through him" (Romans 8:37).

This overcoming love of God doesn't ignore or bypass resistance and its roots in sin. In love he meets me and gently but firmly leads me to see where I resist him so that he might bring light, forgiveness and transforming power into those hidden pockets of resistance. He insists that I participate in the love that redeems me, giving me the motivation and courage to do so even when I am fearful, despondent or reluctant.

In my own journey into God's love and intimacy, I have had to own and name specific forms of resistance. For some years I worked hard to change my unacceptable behaviors and put on more acceptable behaviors that I found in Scripture and was taught in my evangelical subculture. I was a committed follower of Jesus, giving my life in service to him. Yet with more light on what a life of love looked like, I began to see that I was falling far short, and what was worse, I came to see that underneath my good acts were bad motives.

My first significant insight was that as a man I feared love. Love seemed to make me weak, noncompetitive and an easy target. I feared that love would make me less of a man in the eyes of others. Overcoming my resistance to love was difficult. In the end, Jesus redefined *masculinity* for me. Jesus was strong and tender; he confronted fearlessly yet was quick to feel compassion. He allowed nails to be driven into his hands without complaint but readily wept over the pain of his friends. In my frequent and sustained meditation on the Jesus of the Gospels, God patiently overcame my resistance based on my view of myself as man.

Similarly, I discovered that I very much wanted to impress others with how spiritual and dedicated I was. I realized that my overworking and addictive attachment to ministry had roots in my insatiable hunger for achievement, recognition and praise from others. I had to keep working hard to maintain the image that sustained my positive self-assessment. I found myself becoming weary, fragile and angry. I felt like a hypocrite. Outwardly, I served God and others; inwardly, I felt guilt, shame and despair.

I was envious and threatened by the gifts and successes of others, especially colleagues. I was critical of them and uneasy around them, feeling shown-up by their devotion and successes. Obviously I couldn't love them, for I feared them. Along the same lines, I found that I was most deeply hurt and angered when I perceived that others didn't recognize my gifts, achievements or contributions. Being passed over or ignored evoked hurt and anger, so much so that some relationships have remained damaged for years. I could "forgive" them but couldn't let go of the anger I felt toward them.

I also discovered that I was reluctant to receive from others. Jesus commands us to "love one another" and continues to love us through those who serve us for his sake. To know his love fully, we must be willing to receive. I agreed with the concept, but I was a loner. All my relationships were "one way"—I always was the giver—which boosted my ego since it showed that spiritually I was doing better than others. It was many years before I discovered, to my embarrassment, that I wouldn't let myself be vulnerable to others—especially to other men. I didn't want to appear weak and needy. My image was at stake.

Finally, after years of me teaching about giving and receiving love, God gave me grace to own up to the hidden motivations behind my service for him. I woke up to the reality that though I had many acquaintances, I didn't have any real male friends. When the loneliness grew painfully strong, I looked around and saw no one to get close to. I proposed to a friend that we meet regularly to share our lives, but I found that I didn't know how or wasn't able to really open up to him.

A major step away from my resistance to the way of love and toward the kind of joyful love practiced by others came when I sought out a spiritual director, a Catholic priest in Mexico. I found it painful and awkward to risk sharing my needs, and to receive insights and grace from another man, but over time it opened a big window for God's light, which allowed me to clearly see my own brokenness and ingrained sinful patterns and the distorted views of God that operated under the radar of my theology. My spiritual director firmly but gently helped me to experience the theology of grace that I held to so tenaciously but actually knew little about. The seed that was planted through his loving presence with me grew into a much greater openness to receive from many others. Not surprisingly, learning to receive God's love from others also taught and helped me to offer it much more humbly, compassionately and wisely.

GOD'S LOVE OVERCOMES AND TRANSFORMS

God helped me to see and own these things so that I could know that his forgiveness, acceptance and love are deeper, broader and higher than all the disappointing things I saw in myself. In spite of my negative thoughts about how he should think and feel about me, God loves me with an everlasting love. Most importantly and powerfully, he shows me that my value comes from his love, not from my efforts or from others' evaluations; neither is it diminished by my failures or others' actions. I am forever safe in his love.

The greatest proof that I can never be separated from God's love is the death of Jesus on the cross. John says: "This is love: not that we loved God, but that he loved us and sent his Son as an atoning sacrifice for our sins" (1 John 4:10). Paul similarly says: "But God demonstrates his own love for us in this: While we were still sinners, Christ died for us" (Romans 5:8). I vividly remember standing before a representation of Jesus on the cross and sensing that he was addressing me with outstretched arms, saying, "See, this is how much I love you, and because of my death for you nothing can separate you from my love. Don't ever despair." I know the theology of his atoning death, and I know a taste of the awesome love behind it all. In spite of all I (and others) can throw up against myself, the one who has the final word, both now, every day and forever, is Jesus, "the Son of God, who loved me and gave himself for me" (Galatians 2:20). This redeeming love has become the theme of my life and ministry. A stanza from an old hymn by William Cowper (1731-1800) is a song my heart often returns to:

> E'er since, by faith, I saw the stream
> Thy flowing wounds supply,
> Redeeming love has been my theme
> and shall be till I die.[1]

As the Holy Spirit works the knowledge of that love into the core of my being, I see deep change happening, and love beginning to bear its fruit. Resistance weakens; once hard and objectionable "commands" become desirable; self-rejection loses its power; fear and shame recede; and God's presence becomes a delight. Intimacy becomes more authentic— more of me is opened up to God. I can only rejoice, give thanks and join John in worship:

> To him who loves us and has freed us from our sins by his blood, and has made us [yes, even me] to be a kingdom and priests to serve his God and Father—to him be glory and power for ever and ever! Amen. (Revelation 1:5-6)

4

THE PAST

HEALING THE WOUNDS

Gordon Dalbey

He will turn the hearts of the fathers to their children,

and the hearts of the children to their fathers;

or else I will come and strike the land with a curse.

MALACHI 4:6

While leafing through the June 1995 issue of *Men's Health* at the barbershop, I was startled to find, behind cover articles on pumping iron and improved sex, an editorial on page 86 titled "Our Fathers." Young, presumably healthy and on top of his game editing such a popular men's journal, the editor, Joe Kita, was nevertheless grieving the loss of his father, who had died two years earlier. "I'm still waiting for my father to talk to me about sex and success, money and marriage, religion and raising kids," he confessed. "I don't know a man my age who doesn't feel like he's navigating his life without a map."

Having ministered to men around the world, I've found that the average man is not lacking in health, intelligence, talent, energy, desire to succeed and often education as well. But without a father's input, he lives as if sailing a well-designed ship upon a vast sea with no map. And so the man either doesn't know where he's going, or if he does, he doesn't know how to get there.

Just as life requires input, manhood requires fathering. The father shapes a boy's sense of himself more deeply than any other person in his life. Even the father's absence, whether emotional or physical, has destructive effects. There are two ways, after all, to kill a plant: You can cut it down or just not water it.

In a graphic example, Catholic priest Richard Rohr tells the story about a nun ministering in a men's prison. One day early in May, an inmate asked the nun if she could get him a Mother's Day card. Happy to oblige, the nun went into town and bought it for him.

The inmate told others, and the word spread like wildfire around the prison. Soon, dozens of prisoners were knocking on the chaplain's office door asking for their own Mother's Day card. Overwhelmed, the nun wisely thought to call Hallmark's national office for help. The company graciously donated a thousand cards to the prison, and a week before Mother's Day, the prison warden invited inmates to go to the chaplain's office for their cards. By the end of the day, all the cards had been distributed.

The nun was delighted. Soon after this great success, she was looking ahead on her calendar and noted Father's Day just ahead. Planning ahead this time, she again contacted Hallmark, who sent her a thousand Father's Day cards. The warden repeated his announcement the Sunday before Father's Day. "Father's Day came, and Father's Day went," the nun reported in dismay. "Not one inmate asked me for a Father's Day card." She returned all of the cards, unused.[1]

From well-off editor to prison inmate, the father wound that developed in a man's boyhood festers within and among men today. In order for both the individual man and society itself to become as God intends, a man's past must be transformed, beginning with the healing of his father wound.

This brokenness between fathers and sons doesn't only cripple individual men. As the prophet Malachi warned thousands of years ago, it brings a curse on the larger society as well, as godly, masculine deeds of strength, compassion and innovation are supplanted by passivity, anger, and destruction. Short of a time machine, no natural human power can overcome this curse. Therefore, as Malachi prophesied, God sent his Son to heal this wound between fathers and sons, and thereby, to restore relationship between a man and Father God.

Every little boy naturally sees his seemingly all-powerful dad as God. All dads, however, are human beings, and as such, sinful creatures. Inevitably we hurt our sons. If the son doesn't face this wound and take it to Jesus—who reveals the true Father of all men—his disillusion with Dad festers and manifests later in adulthood as either a desperation to please his father or a vengeance to punish him. The wounded son either denies his wound and runs toward Dad or spotlights it and runs rebelliously away. Either way, the kingdom of God suffers.

Focusing exclusively on the earthly father, both responses ignore the young man's own unique destiny and detour him from the call of Father God. Instead, he's trapped in a life of either shameful failure—since no boy can ever imagine measuring up to Dad—or destructive anger. Both the corporate "yes man" and the violent gang member actually stem from this same father wound, each lacking in the creative accomplishment that the Creator and Father of all men ordains.

Because all dads are imperfect, every man has a father wound. Clearly, not all of us act it out destructively enough to go to prison—or at least, to get caught. For most of us it's a nagging shame that we don't have the stuff of manhood. This shame stirs great fear; as every man knows, if other men find out you're weak, you're thrown off the team and cast into outer darkness. And so we're desperate to find that manly "stuff," and will pay whatever the cost to whoever promises to give it to us.

Indeed, the one who can deliver us from the shame of unmanliness properly becomes our Savior and Deliverer. If we don't recognize the Father revealed in Jesus as the true source of manhood, if we don't turn to him for his saving acceptance and healing, our desperation for deliverance clouds our vision and impels us toward counterfeits. Sexual encounters, alcohol, endless TV ballgames, overworking, legalistic religion—the list of compulsive efforts to save ourselves from shame is as long as a man's natural energy allows.

MARBLES FROM DAD

How does a man recognize the father wound of his past, and where does he go for healing?

My own father was a career Naval officer and was assigned to the Pentagon when I was in the fifth grade. On the playground during recess at my new school, I found several boys in my class shooting marbles. Wanting to join them, I walked up to one group as they knelt around the circle of string. "Can I play?" I asked.

"Sure," one boy replied amiably. "Where's your marbles?"

"'My marbles'?" I echoed, confused.

"Yeah," the boy declared, as the group paused to look up at me. "Go ahead and put in your marbles, and you can play!"

"Uh, well . . ." I stammered, "I don't have any marbles."

Shrugging their shoulders, the group matter-of-factly turned away from me and back to their game.

Later that night, I told my father I needed some marbles in order to play with the other boys, and he took me out to buy some. The next day, I put my marbles in the circle and was accepted into the game, certified as one of the boys.

In a larger sense every boy goes to his father for the "marbles" that will gain him both self-acceptance as a man and acceptance among men. Out of that security the father provides his son with a map to manhood. For example, he encourages the boy's talents and passions, as in patting his son on the shoulder and saying "I'm proud of you!" He warns the boy about dangers and harmful influences such as drugs, premarital sex, and legalistic religion. At an appropriate time he talks helpfully to the boy about God's gift of sex, providing a centeredness amid the mysterious, overwhelming attraction that seizes a boy's body even when he sleeps.

Most important, the father connects his son to the Father "from whom all fatherhood in heaven and on earth derives its name" (Ephesians 3:15, with footnote)—by praying with his boy, taking him to church, reading the Bible with him, and taking him to Jesus for praise amid life's joys and centeredness amid its pain and disappointment.

These are some of the major marbles a boy needs to play the game of life successfully.

SON OF THE BEATLES

A father's job is to watch for what God is doing in his child and bless it—to give encouraging voice to what God is calling the boy to become. An unfathered man therefore often has trouble finding his calling in life and developing his special talents and abilities to fulfill it. He may move from job to job, even woman to woman, never knowing what really satisfies because he doesn't know what's "really me." When a man abdicates his calling as a father, the world suffers the effects.[2]

Julian Lennon, son of the late Beatles pop idol John Lennon, is a classic example. In his early twenties, Julian made his musical debut with a best-selling album. Then, to everyone's shock, he suddenly stopped recording altogether. Seven years later, when he finally released a second album, he talked with a reporter about struggling to find his calling.

Julian's mother and father had divorced when he was five, and after that he saw his father, John, perhaps a dozen times. "He walked out the bloody door and was never around," Julian snapped. "I'd admire him on TV—listen to his words and opinions. But for someone who was praised for peace and love and wasn't able to keep that at home, that's hypocrisy."

As the reporter notes, "Julian became a self-taught musician. His father never gave him a music lesson." In the son's words, "We sat down once and maybe he played five chords—that was that. . . . The only thing he ever taught me was how not to be a father."

His hate for his father blinded Julian Lennon to his own calling, and the world suffered the loss of his talent for seven years. As the reporter concluded:

Blood. Talent. Julian has slowly learned to view these as gifts. And by coming to terms with his father's failures, he's felt a freedom to explore the legacies that live within him.

"He spent many years trying to sound like anyone but John Lennon," [rock music author] Gary Graff noted; "now he's at peace sounding like his father, and it's a much more genuine musical statement."[3]

The father not only defines a boy's past, therefore, but also stands at the gateway to his destiny. Coming to terms with your father's failures is an essential task of manhood, required in order to recognize and fulfill your purpose in life. A man must face what his earthly father did *not* give him and grieve that awful loss in order to cry out for it at last from his true, heavenly Father.

The prophetic promise that overcomes the curse found in Malachi is that Jesus has come to heal this father wound by leading a man to know his true Father, apart from his earthly dad. This confidence overcomes a man's natural shame of inadequacy and enables him to become the man he was created to be.

The apostle Paul proclaimed:

I keep asking that the God of our Lord Jesus Christ, the glorious Father, may give you the Spirit of wisdom and revelation, so that you may know him better. I pray also that the eyes of your heart may be enlightened in order that you may know the hope to which he has called you, the riches of his glorious inheritance in the saints, and his incomparably great power for us who believe. That power is like the working of his mighty strength, which he exerted in Christ when he raised him from the dead and seated him at his right hand in the heavenly realms. (Ephesians 1:17-20)

One of the simplest yet greatest "marble" blessings a father can offer to facilitate his son's destiny is simply to enjoy him. When the boy enters the room, for example, Dad's face lights up. He turns away from his ball game, computer, workbench, client or newspaper and rushes to hug his son. A boy who is not enjoyed by his father learns "I'm not much to get excited about." He doubts his place in life, discounts his gifting and calling, and in adulthood shies away from significant accomplishments.

Jesus' Father enjoyed him and freely told the world so. After being baptized by John the Baptist, Jesus emerged from the water and a dove came down from heaven to the Father's joyful outburst, "This is my Son, chosen and marked by my love, delight of my life" (Matthew 3:17 *The Message*).

Significantly, *all of Jesus' accomplishments came after this blessing, not before.* Too often, fathers withhold affirmation from their sons for not performing well when their affirmation is precisely what would lead the boy to do his best.

The father wound, in fact, is most often a wound of absence, of longing for something you didn't get. As such, it's harder to spot than any bruise on your skin. "How can you say I have a father wound?" one man asked me. "I hardly even had a father. He was rarely around, and when he was, he never did much with me."

Without the "marbles of manhood" from Dad, a boy grows up doubting not only his place in the world but his own manhood as well. He's left with a gnawing, empty fear that he doesn't belong among men or measure up in their presence—indeed, that his natural, heartfelt need for affirmation and acceptance is not only insignificant but in fact disqualifies him for manhood. He learns to fear the very man he looks up to and thereby to associate respect with fear rather than with trust. Often, he balks at growing into manhood himself, not only because he feels inadequate but also because he doesn't want to intimidate and hurt others as his father did him.

This resulted in the hippie generation of the 1960s, in which I sought manhood. My father's generation had suffered through a national economic depression in the 1930s, only to face the demands of World War II as young men. Jobs and even food were scarce, as were compassion and assistance. Amid such life-threatening circumstances, feeling pain or fear was deemed counterproductive and scorned as unmanly and therefore shameful. Like my dad when he was a boy, and his father before him, I learned to stuff my feelings and stand quietly alone if I wanted to be seen as strong among older men.

Along with most young men my age, I felt inadequate as a man and was ashamed to tell anyone about it. This charade crippled me in friendships and dating; how can you respect and listen to someone else's heart if no one has taught you to respect and listen to your own?

Once, in my late twenties, a woman I had thoughtlessly wounded asked me in dismay, "When did you cry last?" I stood silent, but not strong—in fact, ashamed and confused—because I couldn't remember when I had last risked such an honest human emotion.

In order to counter the soldiering and emotional disengagement of the older men who had wounded us, my generation of flower children marched under the banner of "peace and love." But this self-righteous veneer merely covered the fact that we had no idea what true peace is or how to love another person. In my rebellious anger I trashed all that my father held dear. He was a Naval officer; I marched for peace. He lived in a suburb, ate Wheaties, drove a Chevy and saluted the flag; I crashed in communes, ate granola, drove a beat-up VW Bug and scorned everything American.

Eventually, the hippie confusion and desperation gave way to the more vengeful slogan "Bring the war home; kill your parents." In that, we had become the very hardened men we protested, and no closer than they to genuine manhood. Killing your father doesn't make you a man;

it only makes you an orphan—the chief prey for the father of lies.

In fact, most of our political and cultural clashing of the 1960s—its in-your-face lifestyles and radical philosophies that fester even today, from pot-smoking to Gay Pride parades—were a fraud, a desperate smokescreen to hide the shame and anger of an abandoned little boy longing for his father.

FLOWER CHILDREN WITHOUT JESUS

A man who hates his father will eventually hate his own manhood. Unable to affirm himself as a man, he can become confused in his gender identity, unable to see clearly what he's been created to do and unwilling to exercise God-given authority to do it. Wounded by older men in authority, he may equate authority with coercion and repression rather than protection and guidance. So he will distrust all authority, even his own—and perhaps especially, that of any god called "Father." Such a man abandons not only himself but also others who need his strength.

As flower children, my generation tried to escape adult responsibility and recapture the innocence of childhood—which our fathers' history had never allowed us and now our own destructive lifestyle threatened to disallow us as well. Without Jesus, we couldn't access the true Father (see John 14:1-14) and discover at last that we are his children. Without Jesus to bear our shame, we could only fabricate a false flowers-and-bare-feet innocence to cover it. Thus we degenerated into the very hardness we protested in the older men—numbing ourselves with drugs and casual sex, and cursing those who differed from us.

In the 1960s God was calling a generation of men to deal with the manly needs that decades of depression and world wars had eclipsed. In a world tired of war, God was calling for a generation of spiritual warriors to overcome such demonic strongholds as militarism, materialism, racism, sexism, and shame-based religion. But instead of confessing honestly "I need you, Daddy" and grieving our loss, my generation masked our pain and anger behind righteous political principles.

We lost our war because we lost the boy—and with him we lost our hearts and the ability to be real. And so we abdicated our occasion to be real men.

Today, the awful legacy of that cowardice is the man-hating spirit that fuels the politically correct value system. In this worldview, ideology has replaced relationship, and masculine values like truth-telling and victory are replaced by tolerance—even tolerance for a wide range of harmful behaviors explicitly proscribed in the Bible. It's grace without truth.

RELIGIOUSLY CORRECT

On the conservative end of the spectrum, men may become Christians and join churches. But too often we manifest the same fear of relationships and become instead religiously correct, striving to measure up to biblical principles, Christian standards of manhood or marks of a spiritual champion.

In our hearts we know that, as the apostle Paul said, "I have the desire to do what is good, but I cannot carry it out" (Romans 7:18). But instead of trusting the Father as sons and getting real with him and each other about our brokenness, we're often too busy trying to cover our shame by preaching moral law and the evils of liberalism. It's truth without grace.

Jesus, meanwhile, reveals the true Father. In that process, he's not about being correct but being real. "For the law was given through Moses," John declared; "grace and truth came through Jesus Christ" (John 1:17). That is, the Father sent Moses to tell us what to do, but he sent Jesus to show us Who does it.

As the Son of God, Jesus came to restore us as sons of the Father. Without Jesus, however, we don't know who we are because we can't know Whose we are. Trying to hide our shame, we define ourselves by what we accomplish and even by who we are not rather than by Whose we are and what he has done.

Transformation of your past begins as you are born again: from a son of the flesh—that is, of your earthly father—to a son of the Spirit. "A man is born physically of human parents," Jesus said, "but he is born spiritually of the Spirit" (John 3:6 TEV). This spirit of sonship transforms your past—precisely as it frees you not to "do it right" but rather to be real enough to recognize God as your true Father and cry out for him to do it in you (see Romans 12:2; Ephesians 3:20; Philippians 2:12-13).

BREAKING THE CYCLE

Liberal or conservative, like the generations of men before us, we've all abandoned the little boy in our hearts. His desperate cry in the wilderness terrifies men who don't trust any father to respond. God, however, has provided for just this need: "Though my father and mother forsake me," the psalmist proclaims, "the LORD will receive me" (Psalm 27:10).

Before doctors can treat a disease, they need to note its effects and diagnose it. However, men don't go to the doctor until they know they're sick, and sometimes it's too late. A society that regards imperfection and brokenness as shameful wants to hide its wounds. The first step toward healing wounds of the past—by admitting their presence and their effects—can be the most difficult.

As the great Physician, Jesus was sent into the world not "to condemn the world, but to save the world" (John 3:17). In order to let God heal us as men, we need first to recognize our wound and spot its effects among us.

Certainly, our sin nature is at the root of all ungodly behaviors. You can't blame Dad or anyone else for that, no matter how badly they've hurt you. But like maggots, your sin nature feeds off your past wounds and can't be checked apart from our Father's healing.

HONORING THE FATHER WHO WOUNDS YOU

The father wound is the hook that our Father uses to draw us to himself. The man who can see clearly what his earthly dad did not give him will be more apt to ask God for it. "In their suffering," the Father hopes, "they will try to find me" (Hosea 5:15 TEV).

Yet we often deny our wound because we're taught to be strong, and a wound feels weak and shameful. "I don't understand all this talk about father wounds," one corporate sales executive complained to me. "I had a good dad and I know he loved me." Later, as our conversation turned to other topics, the man mentioned that during his boyhood, his father had been in prison for several years.

Too often Christian men who recognize their childhood wound are afraid to talk about it for fear of disobeying the commandment "Honor your father and your mother, so that you may live long in the land the LORD your God is giving you" (Exodus 20:12). But as Malachi prophesied, this is precisely the wound that Jesus came to heal. Jesus is the means; the Father is the goal: "No one comes to the Father except through me," Jesus declared (John 14:6).

A man who hides his father wound, whether from shame or fear of being disobedient, will not find good news in this work of Jesus. "My dad was basically OK, so I don't need a heavenly Father," he imagines. What he's really saying is, "I don't trust that there's any other father out there who either loves me enough or is powerful enough to make up for what my natural father did or did not do."

I know I can't give my son all he needs from me as a father. That's why I work at connecting him to our Father God—praying with him, talking about the Scriptures and showing him how I approach God myself when I blow it or otherwise need him. I want my son to honor me for who I am, not for some fantasy that I'm not.

You don't have to curse your parents to acknowledge how they hurt you; you just have to tell the truth and want to get on with your life— that is, to "live long in the land the LORD your God is giving you" (Exodus 20:12).

A hidden wound festers, infects and kills. It doesn't honor me if my son whitewashes my sin or otherwise pretends I'm perfect; it only hurts him. I'm honored and encouraged when he trusts me enough to come and tell me when I hurt or disappoint him. Until he faces my imperfections, he'll never let go of me to seek and know his true and perfect Father—the one, in fact, "from whom all fatherhood in heaven and on earth derives its name" (Ephesians 3:15).

FORGIVENESS THE KEY

Forgiveness is the key to releasing the pain of your past and freeing yourself from its shame and fear. Denial short-circuits this process. A man who fancies *My parents never hurt me* cannot forgive them, simply because he imagines he has nothing to forgive them for.

In learning to forgive, you can ask Jesus to "show me my father the way you see him." Have some tissues on hand when you do. When he asked this of Jesus, one thirty-five-year-old assistant pastor whose dad had been absent during his childhood declared, "I see a little boy on crutches!" Thanking Jesus for this revelation, he asked for more understanding and then burst into tears. "Oh, I see Grampa hurting Dad as a boy too!" At once, he began sobbing tears for his father's boyhood pain. This was a major step toward releasing his masculine energies formerly bottled up in resentment. Feeling your wounder's pain is tantamount to forgiving him; it's hard to hate someone when you're crying for him.

When a man abandons his son, whether physically or emotionally, the son thinks it's because he's a bad boy. Most often, however, it's because the father thinks he himself is a bad man. A good indication of how much your father needs healing is how badly he has wounded you. Instead of cursing your dad, pray for him. A boy, that is, cries *from* his father's wounds. A man cries *for* his father's wounds as an intercessor.

Much of your father wound has simply been passed down through past generations and ultimately came through your dad's own brokenness. Parents are not saints—but neither are they demons. Often, they're just fellow victims of their own childhood wounding. Most parents do the best they can, no matter how little that might be. It's not that they deliberately withheld love; they never received any to give away.

Still, our sinful human nature has its own designs in every generation, and sometimes people, even parents, flat-out choose to hurt you. This is harder to forgive. But that's why Jesus came—to give us God's power to do what we can't.

Holding on to your anger not only perpetuates the wound, but it also destroys the generation after you. As one eighty-plus-year-old declared at one of my men's conferences, "Whatever you don't forgive your father for, you'll do to your son."

Cry out to Jesus for his grace to forgive your father. Then, in your prayer closet or with a trusted friend, say out loud, "Dad, I forgive you for (name the sin against you) and lay down all right to pay you back." Then pray for your father, asking our Father God to heal and bless him. Surrender to Father God your right to confront Dad personally; the real proof of your forgiveness is (1) your willingness to honor him, (2) the peace in your heart, and (3) a growing sense of purpose in your own life.

DAD'S GOOD QUALITIES

One way to honor your father, and thereby invest in your future, is to thank God for Dad's good qualities—and claim these as part of your legitimate heritage. At my conferences, after the first teaching session, I put the men into small groups and say, "Tell the other men your father's finest character trait and something he did to demonstrate that."

Often, men are surprised at the positive memories that emerge and the new confidence they feel. Just as cursing your father curses your own manhood, honoring your father builds you up. After all, every boy looks up to Daddy and wants experience to justify that; if Daddy is good, it follows that I, his son, am also good.

Ask God to recall any ways your father might have affirmed or otherwise blessed you. Often, fathers tell others how much they care about their son, but they don't tell the son himself. You may need to ask aunts and uncles what Dad said about you.

It doesn't have to be his words. I remember the thrill when my father first let me drive his car by myself; he never said much beyond instructions, but his trust in me allowed me to trust myself and drive well. If your father wasn't present in your childhood, maybe your grandfather, uncle or stepfather blessed you. Maybe it was a coach, teacher or boss. Dig deeply into your past for any manly affirmation, and soak it in.

Finally, get on your knees and ask, "Father God, show me myself the way you see me." As Paul put it, the goal is to become one whose praise "is not from men, but from God" (Romans 2:29).

For readers who are dads, consider the power of your words to bless your children and free them from the world's shame. As the late President Kennedy recalled, "If I walked out on the stage and fell flat on my face, Father would say I fell better than anyone else."[4]

In fact, honoring your father like this prepares you for true worship—which is essentially bragging on your heavenly Daddy by proclaiming his goodness and greatness. A man who can sing out "My Daddy is the best!" is uplifted as a man. In that surrender and praise, a man opens his heart to his true Father at last, so the Father can heal through "open-heart" surgery.

A REAL MAN IS A MAN WHO'S REAL

The next step in letting Father God transform your past is critical. When you've humbly faced your ungodly behaviors and asked the Father to heal your wounds, it's time to move beyond the hospital into the barracks—that is, from your own pain into the company of men who are fellow warriors. For this step you need a platoon of brothers battling with you on the journey to manhood. You need men who have suffered the powers of sin and death and who in the midst of that battle have cried out to Jesus and tasted his victory—men who want so badly to overcome their own sin and to heal their wounds that they don't have any energy or desire to judge others.

A real man is a man who's real. He's not trying to cover up his mistakes or pretend he's either better or worse than he is. He wants to discover his created purpose in life and get to the root of what's keeping him from it. Getting real with God by facing your wounds is the first step. But getting real with other men is the terrifying but promising leap that puts you where the Father can do his refining work.

Jesus told his followers, "I and the Father are one" (John 10:30). Furthermore, he promised that "where two or three come together in my name, there am I with them" (Matthew 18:20). The Father is the source of manhood. To meet the Father, you must encounter Jesus. A man can do this by meeting regularly and getting real with two or three other men who have surrendered their lives to Jesus.

It's simple, but it's not easy for most men today. A boy, after all, learns what it's like to be around other men by being with his father. A boy who has not had a father at home or whose father has been emotionally distant will feel anxious about getting real with other men; it's unfamiliar, even dangerous territory. He longs for their acceptance but is afraid they won't give it to him—as it was with Dad.

SEEK YOUR PLATOON

Decades ago, when my professional and family life was in turmoil, I became overwhelmed with fear. In desperation, I finally mustered the courage to call four other men and say to each, "I need you." For several years we met in my office every Friday morning at 7 a.m. We agreed to be real together, and not to share anything said in the group with anyone outside the group. Before long, what had started as a fearful leap of faith became a rock-solid base for growing into manhood.

Sex and marriage, money and job, faith and failures—we talked about it all and prayed it through. Knowing we were all struggling in these areas took the sting of shame away and allowed us to stay real and open to the Father. Sure, I still had to face many trials alone—but I was prepared to do so.

If you want to honor your father so you can occupy "the land the LORD your God is giving you," get your platoon together.

TIME WITH THE FATHER

In order to know someone, you need to spend time with him or her. In this painful season, I wanted to know my true, heavenly Father, so I blocked out time early each morning to be with him. Crying out for his truth and grace, I eagerly read his words in the Scriptures, sometimes just flipping the pages here and there, other times going through the *One Year Bible,* reading a few passages daily. I typed verses on index cards and memorized those that especially grabbed me.

After reading, I would kneel before a small cross on my desk and offer myself to the Father, asking him to show me my own sin so I could repent, to show me where others had sinned against me so I could seek healing, to show me what he was doing in my life so I could cooperate. I kept a journal, writing down Scriptures, impressions, words, dreams and experiences that stirred me.

Determined not to waste this painful ordeal, I sought out Christian counseling, went to conferences and workshops on biblically based healing, read related books, worshiped to praise tapes, and prayed and prayed and prayed some more. Bottom line: tell the Father what you're fed up with, give him full permission to do whatever's necessary to overcome it, and put yourself where he can.

HONOR YOUR BODY

During this season of upset and restoration, I decided for the first time to honor my male body. I cut out high-fat foods like whole milk, potato chips, French fries, cheeseburgers, hot dogs, ribs and the like, and began to eat more broiled and baked chicken, turkey and fish, whole-grain bread and cereals, and fresh vegetables, fruit and nuts. I've worked at cutting back on sugar, which has been harder. (When you've got the urge, nothing seems to satisfy like a chocolate chip cookie!)

Besides eating healthier, I began working out regularly—using a variety of exercises so I didn't overwork any body part. Jogging, weightlifting, cycling, tennis, basketball and fast-walking refresh me. A good sweat and shower can release a lot of stress and help toward a good night's sleep. During particularly stressful days, I discovered that it was helpful to concentrate on hitting or shooting a ball rather than participating in a sport that let my mind wander, as in jogging.

The important thing is to find reasonably enjoyable workouts that fit your own needs. Overall, I try to be sensible about my diet and exercise. If I'm too hard on myself, it just stirs the old sabotaging rebel in me.

Exercising regularly isn't always easy. Busy schedules and family needs, not to mention just plain laziness, crowd in at times. But if you're too busy to exercise, you're too busy. Your body is not just a work machine or some lower form of creation; it's the temple of the Holy Spirit (1 Corinthians 6:19), the vehicle of the Father's work in and through you in this world. Jesus had a body; honor yours accordingly.

AN ONGOING PROCESS

If you do all these things, will those old wounds of the past forever disappear from your mind? Probably not. But that's all part of God's plan too. Transformation of your past is an ongoing process of drawing closer to the Father.

Bringing your wounds to Jesus removes their sting so they no longer have power to cripple you in working out your calling. But totally removing them from your memory is not a realistic goal—not because God wants you to suffer but because his purposes are greater than simply removing your discomfort. Jesus didn't come to make religious robots through a holy lobotomy that erases all memory of pain. He came to call forth sons who learn through suffering to draw close to the Father (2 Timothy 2:3).

Biblically speaking, the past is neither "used up" time to be discarded nor a hobby for history buffs, but the theater where God reveals his character and purposes. On the cross, God demonstrated that his ultimate purpose is not to remove our pain and suffering but to use our wounds to prepare us for his future calling. The trusting relationship with him that emerges from this process is what defines healing—not the removal of pain.

The promise in this Father-son relationship is a lifestyle of purpose and transforming power—not only for yourself but for others as well. Your past is transformed when, like Jesus on the cross, you can give its brokenness to the Father and let him use it for his larger purposes in this broken world.

The apostle Paul explains: "Praise be to the God and Father of our Lord Jesus Christ, the Father of compassion and the God of all comfort, who comforts us in all our troubles, so that we can comfort those in any trouble with the comfort we ourselves have received from God" (2 Corinthians 1:3-4).

What then are the signs that a man's past is being transformed?

He's willing to risk being real with himself, with the Father and with other men. He wants the truth, the whole truth and nothing but the truth, no matter how painful, fearful or shameful. He's realizing that he exits for a purpose, that only his true Father—revealed historically in Jesus and present today in the Holy Spirit—can fulfill that purpose in and through him. He wants to trust the Father and surrender daily to him. In fact, God has set the agenda for each man and "has given us everything we need for life and godliness through our knowledge of him who called us by his own glory and goodness" (2 Peter 1:3).

Growing in faith is not about what *you* do but about what *God* does in you. If godly manhood were just about behavior change, Moses and his law would have been enough. But the Father doesn't want your sacrifices, that is, your efforts to prove how capable and good you are. Rather, he wants "a broken and contrite heart" (Psalm 51:17), which allows him to prove how capable and good he is in your life. He sent Jesus to do the sacrificing for us so we could concentrate on receiving his grace—and thereby be transformed from slaves to the law to grateful and loyal sons.

Transformation of a man's past means growing from a childish fear of not doing it right before men to a son's confidence in being real before his Father. "For you did not receive a spirit that makes you a slave again to fear," Paul admonished the Roman church, "but you received the Spirit of sonship. And by him we cry, 'Abba, Father' " (Romans 8:15).

May we be so transformed as men.

5

FAILURE

EXPLORING THE BENEFITS

Robert A. Fryling

Y*ou're fired!* With a dismissive flick of his wrist and a well-choreographed bounce of his hair, Donald Trump tells his failed wannabes that they no longer have a job on his popular reality show, *The Apprentice*. These firing scenes make for great drama, but real-life times of failure don't fit in so neatly between planned commercial breaks.

Failure for most of us is a messy and traumatic realization that something has gone wrong in our life. For some it is a failed marriage or failed parenting or failure in our Christian life. But for many men our most debilitating times of failure are connected with job loss, because our masculine identity is so strongly associated with our work. We are proud of what we do and what we accomplish. When we lose our role for whatever reason, we become disoriented in who we are. We often feel defensive or inadequate or both. Rarely do we anticipate that failure can be a gateway to spiritual transformation.

Consequently, let me share with you a time of profound job failure for me and how God used this gut-wrenching experience to precipitate a genuine transformation of my heart and life.

BACKGROUND TO FAILURE

I studied metallurgical engineering in college and I did my co-op work with Ford Motor Company. I liked my job. In my senior year Ford made me a great job offer. However, during my college years I was also involved with a campus student ministry, InterVarsity Christian Fellowship. I was our chapter's president and saw God's work both in my own life and in the lives of my classmates. Students were becoming Christians and growing in their faith. I enjoyed being part of their spiritual vitality.

Consequently, upon graduation I reluctantly turned down the offer from Ford and chose to become a campus staff member. Although I believed that God calls most people to the secular marketplace, I sensed that God was calling me to invest my life in students. I loved the university world and the tremendous opportunities for Christian discipleship and witness among students and faculty.

During my first year on staff I met Alice, who was a campus staff member in the nearby Boston area. We both had a love for students— and as it turned out, for each other! We "dated" at staff meetings and student conferences and got married the next year.

Not long after we were married I was asked to become a team leader. This began a fast organizational track for me of taking on more and more responsibilities that led to my being appointed as national director of campus ministry at the age of thirty-two. By then Alice and I had two daughters and our family of four moved from our friends and home in New England to the national offices for InterVarsity Christian Fellowship, in Madison, Wisconsin. I was subsequently appointed vice president and for fourteen successful years I felt that I had the perfect job for the rest of my life.

A quarter turn to the right. Then one day my job and sense of identity imploded. I was leading a Bible study in 1 Corinthians 1 for a group of thirty senior leaders. We were discussing Paul's teaching against divisions and the need for spiritual unity. I chose this passage because we were experiencing tensions and competition between some members of the group. I wanted to solve these problems, hoping others would be convicted of their prideful spirit through the Bible study. What I didn't anticipate was that the solution to our organizational problems would instead begin with me.

What happened was this. In the middle of the Bible study, people started complaining about our organizational dysfunctions. I hoped that verbalizing these problems would lead to a time of confession. It led instead to a time of questioning of our national leadership. Someone obliquely said that we had an unspoken problem we were afraid to address.

By this time I was frustrated and angrily asked whether I was the unspoken problem. I knew as soon as I blurted this out that I had to let them answer this without me in the room. So I asked our president to finish leading the discussion before our mid-morning break and then I left the room.

What I thought would be a twenty-minute vindication of my leadership turned into an all-day discussion, without me in the room, about our entire leadership structure. I learned at midday that my position had been abolished. Our leadership team was stuck, and my role was deemed to be the primary sticking point. This change was described to others as "making a quarter turn to the right" to downplay any fears of a major organizational upheaval. Although that description may have been adequate for others, I was the one who lost my job and I felt very much "upheaved!"

While my job fate was being decided, I had nothing to do for eight hours other than walk and think and wonder about what I had done so wrong as to deserve this painful isolation and rejection. As I walked, I couldn't enjoy the splendor of the fall foliage or the fellowship of colleagues I had worked with for many years. I was alone, awaiting the outcome of their discussions.

I was also confused. I was angry. I was afraid. I was fearful. I felt a mixture of shame, guilt, blame and failure. I wanted to know what had happened so suddenly to me and my career. Where would I go next? What would I say to our friends in church and to all of those on my prayer letter list? What would I tell my parents, my daughters? What would I tell Alice?

What was most troubling, though, was that I felt a silence from God. I wanted to understand why I was losing my job and I wanted God to be both my interpreter and defender. But despite my tearful prayers there was only the sound of silence.

A dark day of the soul. Although I didn't use this terminology that day, what I was experiencing was what the Spanish mystic John of the Cross called the "dark night of the soul." Currently, this expression is sometimes used to describe depression and other negative emotional experiences. The original meaning, however, was more associated with the perceived absence of God rather than just an emotional low. It described a spiritual void, and that is what I felt that day. God seemed either away or unavailable, and I felt abandoned.

Yet even in my discouragement, there were two passages of Scripture that came to mind near the end of the day that gave me hope. First, there were the words of Jesus from the cross: "My God, my God, why have you forsaken me?" (Matthew 27:46). When these words spontaneously formed on my lips, I shuddered because they felt blasphemous for me to utter. The experience of losing my job in no way compared to what Jesus suffered in his death. Yet there was also solace in that what I was experiencing in a very small way was what Jesus had experienced for me. I could trust him as one who had also experienced divine isolation. I was no longer completely alone.

The other passage was also the words of Jesus, this time praying for those who were gathered around his place of execution. "Father, forgive them, for they do not know what they are doing" (Luke 23:34). Here was the profound example of Jesus offering forgiveness to those who had rejected him. When I felt most discouraged, without anyone else in the world who could understand what was happening, the Lord gave me his example and encouragement to follow in his steps.

I saw in Jesus a call to let go of my instinctive attitudes of vindictiveness and self-justification. Instead I was to offer forgiveness. Without this quiet invasion of divine grace that day, I think I would have gone down the path of being bitter about the organization and its leadership. But the path of forgiveness was a road to liberation for me and how I felt about my colleagues. As Henri Nouwen wisely observed, "forgiveness is to allow the other person not to be God."[1]

However, this is not the end of the story. Like many men, I wanted a quick solution to the problem rather than having to live through the problem to a more mature and relational resolution. I hoped forgiveness was a one-time event and change would happen instantaneously. What I learned that day was just the beginning of what I needed to learn about myself and what it means to be transformed.

LEARNING IN MY FAILURE

Although the abolishment of my position was just one piece of what was being addressed in InterVarsity at the time, I have found it helpful to reflect back on what God taught me personally through these organizational changes. In particular, I have learned more about how to *pay attention:* to myself, to others and to God.

Paying attention to myself. When I first joined InterVarsity, I heard someone teach from 1 Timothy 4:16 (NRSV): "Pay close attention to yourself and to your teaching." The application was that I needed not only to study hard and be careful what I taught to students but that I should be disciplined in my personal life—eat right, get exercise, live a clean life and so on. Indeed, I did try to do all of this, but I didn't understand or know what it meant to pay attention to my soul. I was paying attention to what I did and what I thought but was detached from my internal life. I was basically willing to change anything that I could consciously change, but I was unconscious of my spiritual blind spots.

Consequently, my job failure did for me what I couldn't do for myself. Because I was so intentionally trying to do what was right, I was spiritually blocked from seeing what was wrong in me. However, in my time of vocational nakedness I realized how much I had previously clothed myself with an identity that was synonymous with my job. When I lost my job, I also lost what I perceived people thought of me and my value to them. I felt worthless, inadequate and emasculated as a Christian leader.

I was like Gideon in the book of Judges, who went from being a man of faith to allowing his job success to be a focus of idolatry. He gloried in the praise of his followers. Although I consciously tried to be more humble than that, my unconscious soul was quite taken with my own success! My glittering image had been stripped away and the shallowness of my soul was exposed.

An even more vivid image for me is the despicable Gollum in Tolkien's *The Hobbit.* Gollum refers to the magic ring as "my precious." I was deeply shaken when I realized that my job was my ring of power and that it was "my precious." I felt entitled to it because I had worked so hard and had tried to do everything right. My mistake was focusing so much of my life on what I was doing for God rather than on what God wanted to do in me.

Another lesson in self-awareness was realizing how important efficiency is to me. I like to maximize my energies, my time and my job productivity. This was another part of my success. I worked harder and got more done than others, which was visibly recognized in my job promotions. Badness did not seem to be as much of a problem for me as busyness.

However, my job accomplishments sometimes came at the expense of my relationships, especially with those I supervised. I wanted them to be successful so that I could be successful, but deep down I wasn't really invested in them beyond their job role and performance. I thought that my efficiency was just good stewardship; I didn't realize that it also reflected a self-centeredness that gave me power and control. Thomas Merton called efficiency "the leading spiritual disease in our culture."[2] It was only the inefficiency of losing my job that helped me see this relational illness.

I also learned about the incestuous relationship within me between self-pity and overresponsibility. When I was really working hard, I felt tremendous responsibility for not only my own job but everybody else's as well. Unfortunately, I was very prone to feeling self-pity if everything did not go well. I felt that I deserved success and especially recognition for that success. When that didn't happen, I was critical of others and wallowed in self-pity. I experienced what someone has said: "self-pity is the most addictive of all non-pharmaceutical narcotics."

Unfortunately, Alice often bore the brunt of this addiction. At one point she had quietly taped to my desk blotter the wise comment that "to criticize others is a dishonest way of praising yourself." But even though I tried to be more positive toward others, my root problem was not negativity but self-sufficiency. I was presumptuous in thinking I knew best how to perfect my Christian life. Pride kept me from truly knowing myself. It was the humiliation of my job loss that broke through this protective barrier. I saw with new eyes why the psalmist prayed for protection from presumptuous sins (Psalm 19:13).

Much of what I learned through my job crisis were the spiritual convictions and virtues of paying attention to myself in ways that drew me to God. I experienced what John Calvin stated in the very beginning of his *Institutes of the Christian Religion*: "Nearly the whole of sacred doctrine consists in these two parts: knowledge of God and of ourselves."[3] When I lost my job, I also lost my sense of self-sufficiency, which ironically allowed me to pay closer attention to what was really going on inside myself. I was then able to become more in touch with God and with others.

Paying attention to others. As I have already described, a devastating part of failure is the tremendous sense of isolation and loneliness. Although I awkwardly wanted to talk about my loss, I also got tired about talking about what happened. I didn't want to criticize others. I didn't want to either justify or admit to my failures, and I definitely didn't want to talk about my feelings about the whole situation. When I tried to talk about them, the result was rather bland or perfunctory. To be angry would just be another point of failure!

But I couldn't successfully process my failure by myself. As much as I felt isolated and was inclined to process my shattered world privately, I needed the help of others. I needed to pay attention not only to their counsel and encouragement but also to how my situation was affecting them.

The most obvious impact was on Alice. As she felt my pain and sadness' she expressed some of the anger I was avoiding! Yet she was not uncritically defensive of me. She has often said that part of her ministry to me is to "blow up my balloon and when necessary to pop it!" This was definitely a blowing up time, but she also knew that I had blind spots and perhaps this firing was related to them.

We had many long walks together during which she allowed me to talk and to express my fears and deep hurts with others and with myself. She prayed for me and with me, and was gentle with me. She gave me opportunity to talk as well as to be quiet. I deeply benefited from her gifts of spiritual direction and her unfailing love for me. We grew closer together in sharing this vocational crisis.

Alice also supported me as I interviewed for jobs away from our home in Madison. This was tremendously difficult for her because she hates to move, and we both were thoroughly committed to our church. We loved our city, our church, our friends. Our two daughters grew up in Madison, and we didn't want to move!

But when a new job opportunity in the Chicago area came about, Alice was the first one to sense that we needed to go. For her it was a step of faith, like Abraham leaving his home country. For both of us it was a very stressful and emotional time. Our oldest daughter was getting married, our youngest daughter was graduating from college, and my parents were moving to a retirement facility. Our whole family was in transition!

Yet it seemed to be the right decision, and Alice's loyalty and courage were major pieces to making this choice. After our move, though, Alice had major health problems that likely were due to the stress of the whole transition. I am indebted to her for her sacrifice for me. But in God's abundant economy, Alice has since thrived in Chicago and in her spiritual-direction ministry.

Our daughters too, although no longer living in Madison, survived the emotional turmoil with us. I don't think they were ever blinded by the belief that I was perfect, but they too had a certain identity in my identity, and they also felt a loss as we moved away from their church and friends. I had pangs of guilt about that, but we learned that our family love is far stronger than geographical attachments.

I also gained support and strength from those in our church in Madison. The first Sunday after my job loss, I was scheduled to teach an adult education class and I wasn't sure what people would be thinking about me. They didn't know the details of what happened, but I feared that they might be thinking the worst about me. Was I fired because of moral failure or just gross incompetence?!

Perhaps some had such thoughts, but what I received that day was wonderful loving support and care. A friend who normally wasn't in that class came that morning just to be there and pray for me. Some other friends specifically invited me to sit with them during the worship service; others included us in their dinner plans. These expressions of non-judgmental love that continued for months were a valuable part of my healing process. I saw Christian community with the fresh eyes of receiving from others.

One other piece of healing that is not inconsequential happened four years after my job transition. Basically, the same group of senior leaders who had been involved previously in deciding my future planned a dinner for Alice and me. They wanted to thank me for my contributions and to offer an apology for my job-termination process. It seemed that we all had actually failed a bit and needed to pay more attention to each other. This dinner was a valuable cleansing time for all of us and a tribute to God's grace lived out among imperfect believers.

Paying attention to God. As I have already mentioned, I was in a position of significant Christian leadership and was doing good things for God. I prayed, I studied and taught the Bible, and I tried to help others know God better. I was getting paid to pay attention to God, and I honestly tried to do so.

But I wasn't always in touch with God, and I didn't understand the rhythms of the Holy Spirit in my life. I believed that God was in control of all of life but I couldn't accept that he ordained evil or just plain bad things in the world. So I was confused as to whether or not God wanted me fired or just allowed it to happen. I still don't know for sure, but I do know that the Lord, as the potter, worked through this time to shape the clay of my life in deep ways of internal transformation.

TRANSFORMATION THROUGH MY FAILURE

A new job. When I was most disheartened about my job loss, I didn't think it would be possible to remain with InterVarsity. Although there were many other things I could do, I wasn't sure I could find peace and satisfaction when my failure was so visible throughout the organization. So I interviewed outside of InterVarsity and considered various intriguing options. But my heart was not in them.

Then the job opening for a new director of InterVarsity Press stared me in the face. The previous director had to leave prematurely for health reasons and there was an extended search in the publishing industry for his replacement. Although my dad had been in publishing all of his life and I was a lover of books, I had no publishing experience and didn't feel qualified for this role. But at the encouragement of others, I applied for the position and because of my extensive management experience was appointed to my current vocation as publisher of InterVarsity Press.

This was an awkward organizational transition, and it is very awkward writing this chapter! It isn't easy to share my warts as well as the warts of my employer! But these warts are part of my life. They are also now overshadowed by the redemptive work of God in me and in Inter-Varsity. I love my new job. I love books and ideas. I enjoy working with authors and my talented and delightful colleagues. The challenge of publishing books that serve the church with grace and truth is an inspiring vision. Even writing a chapter on failure seems like something with a divine smile behind it! I am very grateful.

A renewed heart. Spiritual transformation for me has not been a one-time event. As the apostle Paul predicted, it is an ongoing process of being conformed to the image of Christ (2 Corinthians 3:18). Being fired from the job I loved was clearly part of this process. My job failure did not transform me per se, but it forced me to look internally and see what was happening in my soul. It was a traumatic testing, but it was also a touch of grace that gave me time to be more intentionally aware of God's transforming work in my life—and especially in my heart.

Since then I have tried to embrace transformation of my heart in four ways: by having (1) a quiet heart, (2) a circumcised heart, (3) a burning heart and (4) a dancing heart. There are many stories behind me choosing or being led to these spiritual affections of my heart, but let me share just a summary of them.

A quiet heart. There is no doubt that my spiritual vitality is directly related to the times of quiet I have to internally rest, reflect and pray. Even early in our marriage, Alice could always tell when I wasn't taking time for a meaningful devotional life because of my negative effect on her. I was either more irritable or detached in my relationship with her and our girls when my soul was not at peace.

But my devotional times were not sufficient in the midst of pressured management decisions. It was hard to be at peace each morning when my whole life was being fueled by high-octane activities and responsibilities. In the time since my job transition I have found great joy and restoration in the practice of sabbath. I try to practice it religiously, but not legalistically!

The key for me is to not have any expectations of having to get any-

thing done on Sunday afternoons after being part of our church community in the morning. I don't sit at my desk to pay bills or to do work for
my job. I save and savor the time for reading, praying and resting. I'm also
usually successful in avoiding TV (yes, even sports). This time of regular
quiet restores me both physically and spiritually, and helps me to be a
faithful but not driven person in my responsibilities the rest of the week.

A circumcised heart. I discovered the cleansing power of cutting away
the things that hindered my spiritual growth as well as the impossibility
of doing it all myself. Because of this I have found great truth in the
promise of God that "The LORD your God will circumcise your hearts . . .
so that you may love him with all your heart and with all your soul, and
live" (Deuteronomy 30:6). This vivid metaphor of pain and tenderness
is a powerful one for dealing with failure. From a human standpoint the
imagery is emasculating, but from an eternal perspective it's a symbol of
divine surgery that provides healing and life.

In response to this, my prayer has been that I would have a circumcised heart that would enable me to be a free person—free from having
to be right, free from having to be responsible for everything, free from
attachments to sports and television and sexual fantasies, free to live life
more open-handedly and not cling to things that used to make me feel
secure. It also means being free from what had been an unconscious
habit of soliciting praise and recognition from others. Circumcision is a
painful operation, but circumcision of my heart has become a necessary
procedure for spiritual transformation.

A burning heart. I have always enjoyed the post-Easter story of the
two disciples on the road to Emmaus and their encounter with the
risen Lord. It is a wonderfully human story of two friends struggling to
understand a very difficult event in life. They were discouraged, confused and consequently unable to recognize Jesus, who was walking
alongside them. Only after the sharing of bread together did they realize that their companion had been Jesus, and they exclaimed "Were not
our hearts burning within us while he talked with us on the road and

opened the Scriptures to us?" (Luke 24:32).

I have used this imagery of a burning heart to capture my desire to pursue God with an emotional intensity that isn't first nature to my engineering mindset. Although I will probably never be nor was I created to be a demonstrative extrovert, I do sense that transformation of my heart does include a deeper stirring of my love for the Lord and his Word. Such a love is not limited to just learning more information but rather experiencing a deeper transformation.

A dancing heart. I believe that spiritual transformation is never limited to just an internal or privatistic experience, no matter how satisfying that might seem. Instead, love for God is tightly paired with a love for neighbor as well. The Great Commandments were designated as such by Jesus and cannot be separated from each other. As a wonderful Japanese friend shared with me in halting English, "To be in the presence of God enables us to be a present for others."

But quite frankly this has been the hardest part of my transformational journey so far. I resonate more with having a quiet heart and a burning heart and even a circumcised heart. They are aspirations that I can more easily control. But loving my neighbor is much more difficult because my "neighbors" at home, at work and in society are also imperfect like I am. It is usually much easier to forgive myself (or rationalize my actions) than to forgive someone else.

The image of dancing, though, has been helpful. It is a picture of exuberance and fullness. So every Sunday, when I pray through these desired affections of the heart I pray that I would be joyful (or full of joy), peaceful (or full of peace), hopeful, graceful and so forth. Like the burning heart, a dancing heart feels a little bit like writing with my emotional left hand when I am emotionally right handed, but it has been perhaps the most exciting part of the transformation process for me. It has given me a much more generous perspective with my family, my colleagues at work and those in need in society and throughout the world. It has taken me from carefully watching others to walking with them.

MY PRAYER

I want to conclude with a personal prayer that I use weekly as part of my sabbath reflections. I offer it as a witness to the work of God in me, through both my successes and failures.

"Lord, grant me a quiet heart that is not distraught with internal regrets or frenzied by external circumstances, but rather finds its peace and satisfaction in you.

"Please circumcise my heart from temporal attachments and entanglements so that I may love you with all of heart, soul, mind and strength, and my neighbor as myself.

"I pray that you would also create in me a burning heart for understanding, obeying and delighting in your Word.

"And grant me a dancing heart of joy that engages the world around me with you and your kingdom.

"Fill me with your Holy Spirit that I may lead and serve others with beauty, wisdom and purpose as an instrument of your grace to the glory of your name. Amen."

6

VOCATION

LISTENING FOR THE VOICE THAT CALLS US

Fil Anderson

It's unimaginable that a book with the transformation of a man's heart as its focus could be written without addressing the topic of vocation. Work can be inspired and praiseworthy as well as vicious and numbing, but regardless of its effect, work is what the vast majority of us have to do much of the time and most of our lives. Some of our lives are enhanced and others depleted by work. Whether the work environment is our home or an office building, industrial plant or retail store, indoors or outside, and whether our dress is formal or casual, many of us leave work less alive, wishing we had more time and energy for those facets of our lives that we enjoy and find more meaningful.

As men who yearn to reflect Paul's words "If anyone is in Christ, he is a new creation; the old has gone, the new has come!" (2 Corinthians 5:17) and "In him we live and move and have our being" (Acts 17:28), these are issues that we must ponder: Do the time and energy we spend working also enrich our lives? Is there a definite link between the huge effort required to maintain our home, contribute to our community, provide for the well-being of our family and the intimacy of our relationship with God? The answer I would offer to each question is, it all depends.

When my identity is enmeshed in my work; when the measure of my worth is my productivity, monetary success or renown; when remaining constantly busy is the thing I do to feel important or to avoid feelings of emptiness; then in all likelihood my work is toxic and hazardous to my health. Whenever I'm looking for myself or trying to escape myself in my work, I'm flirting with that horrible dependence or addiction called workaholism. One very clear symptom of workaholism is being so consumed with work that even when I'm not at work, my mind is working on my work. When this occurs, the things I claim that matter most in my life suffer—relationships, personal health, the perspective needed to enjoy the little things in life, and being able to rest in the awareness that my work is an important means and not an end.

RUNNING ON EMPTY

On many days I've felt like the poster boy for workaholism. I've lived the truth about which I'm writing. In an earlier book, I offered this painful confession:

> Late at night while Lucie and our children slept, I would lie awake fearing that I had come to the end of my rope. My despair was the by-product of the life that I had created for my family and myself. It had not appeared overnight. What finally came crashing down was the result of fifteen years of relentless striving. . . . I had succumbed to the power of my compulsions and illusions. . . . What had driven me from one event to another, one project to another, one relationship to another? Why could I never say no?
>
> These questions would resurface during the rare moments of calm and quiet in my life. . . . Late at night, as my family slept, I couldn't keep hiding. The questions came unbidden, and I knew time was about to run out.

I was more than busy; I was exhausted. At night I was restless—too many of the day's activities would loop through my brain. And the following morning it was all I could do to drag myself out of bed to face the day. I was running on grit and adrenaline. For quite some time I had loved having every moment crammed with activity. More specifically, it was the fuel on which I ran. I loved being in demand. But now I was running on empty.[1]

My crisis was more than a cluster of boundary and time-management issues. Fueling my nonstop pace were some deeply rooted and profoundly distorted ideas about God, myself and the how and why of life. The beginning of my recovery from an addiction to work has involved a total overhaul of my understanding of God's original purpose for giving me work to do. Aware that my identity is rooted in my relationship with God, I've been set free to use my energy, intellect, skill and care as an expression of my identity, the source of which is the Spirit of God who lives within me and whispers to me that I am God's beloved son. Having my identity unmistakably rooted in this remarkable fact, I'm both energized by my work and emanate life through it.

LET'S GET REAL

Work is an inescapable reality. It's what occupies a significant portion of most of our days. It's how we manage to pay our bills. But its significance is much farther reaching. It reflects our unique place in the world as God's created daughters and sons. The crucial question is whether we believe our work is part of God's original plan or a result of the rebellion of God's children.

Most of the world has answered the question about work's purpose and importance: "Burdensome, oppressive, a necessary evil" appears to be the consensus opinion. Most working people believe they work in order to live. Most live in the illusion that pleasure and happiness will come after their work is done. But the happiness and pleasure that come with having no work to do, I suspect is short-lived. Like a steady diet of desserts, idleness gets old after a while. There's a deeper gladness that comes with a job, a project or an occupation that engages my heart, mind and body, and provides me with purpose, meaning, and connection with God and others.

The Bible is clear on the subject of work. "The LORD God took the man," Scripture says, "and put him in the Garden of Eden to work it and take care of it" (Genesis 2:15). Adam was put in the garden to work it, not to sit and ponder it; not to live off of it; not to rest, take naps and play all the time. Even in this ideal world God expected Adam and Eve to work as cocreators with God.

On the other end of biblical history, work is spoken of as a duty. Paul's rule was simple and clear: "If a man will not work, he shall not eat" (2 Thessalonians 3:10). Back again in the book of Genesis, God confronts Adam after his rebellion:

> Cursed is the ground because of you;
> > through painful toil you will eat of it
> > all the days of your life. . . .
> By the sweat of your brow
> > you will eat your food
> > until you return to the ground. (Genesis 3:17, 19)

With this passage as a foundation, some view work as affliction, a punishment for rebellion. But for others, like me, the challenge is to bring together the necessity of work and the longing for intimacy with God.

It's natural to assume that those whose work is related to their passion (for example, athletes, pilots, artists or musicians) can more easily find fulfillment in what they do. But job satisfaction is as much a product of perspective, significance and relationship as it is the use of our skills or talents. We don't necessarily have to find pleasure in the tasks our jobs require in order to be made happy by doing them. "What is important," says Tom Stella,

> is that we are open to the bigger picture wherein we sense that we are a piece of a puzzle and that what we do fits into and contributes

to the whole. Without the miller; no flour. Without the baker, no bread. Without the grocer, no access to the bread. This awareness is related to our consciousness of the Ground of Being, for that Ground is the Essence of the wheat, and the flour, and the bread, and all whose hands are involved in its creation, sale, and consumption.

Therefore, Stella concludes,

> We will find our work satisfying and meaningful not primarily because we enjoy it, are good at it, or become wealthy because of it, but because through it we can express and experience the abiding presence of God, a sense of connection and collaboration with others, and the realization that we are making a needed contribution.[2]

WHAT'S YOUR APPROACH?

The prolific author and monk Thomas Merton was fond of emphasizing that more can be known about a monk by the way he uses a broom than by what he says. Undoubtedly, others can learn a lot about us by the approach we take to our work. When I'm searching the Yellow Pages for a plumber, I'm less interested in a Christian symbol on the ad than the quality of the plumber's plumbing.

When I'm attentive to my work and to God, my approach to both is greatly enhanced. A man who's seeking God in his work and relationships doesn't just "go through the motions." Because spirituality is a down-to-earth matter, spiritual growth is evidenced more by the smell of sweat than by the aroma of "holiness," and more by the calluses on our hands than the growing of wings! When it's God I seek, there's no avoidance of hard work: manual, menial or mental.

Recognizing and keeping God's presence in everything we do is absolutely essential when it comes to living the good life that I believe God intends for each of us. The challenge is to avoid thinking compartmentally about life. Well-meaning friends often ask, "How's your spiritual life?" or "How's your work?" or "How's your marriage?" as if these parts of my life can be kept separate.

St. Benedict offered the body of Christ a useful system to help us examine and arrange our lives. Benedict taught that each day is to be ordered, assuring opportunity for prayer, work, community relations and rest. None was more important or more highly esteemed than another. Each was seen as necessary and good. No division was made between the "secular" and the "spiritual." Benedict understood that there's no artificial division between the sacred domain of prayer and the worldly activity of work. Everything in life is sacred. Rightly understood, prayer is a form of work, and work is a form of prayer.

One of the most challenging and insightful yet overlooked and misunderstood aspects of the creation story occurred when God observed that all the things made were good: "God saw all that he had made, and it was very good" (Genesis 1:31). It's crucial to appreciate that although what God had done was good, creation wasn't yet finished. Instead, God committed the rest of creation to us. Work is our contribution to the ongoing creation of the world and the means wherein we demonstrate that we're made in God's image.

BRINGING THE PRESENCE OF GOD CLOSER

God provided us with an abundant world, a world with plenty of resources and work to be done. God placed us here to work with purpose, integrity, excellence and creativity. Work brings the presence of God closer and continues the work of God through us. Our purpose is not to live long enough or work hard enough to some day retire from work. Work isn't a distraction, curse or diversion from God; it's his gift to us.

No one has offered more practical and clear enlightenment on work than Brother Lawrence of the Resurrection, who entered a monastery in Paris after retiring from military service. Because of his peasant background and lack of formal education, he was assigned to the kitchen. There he spent forty years washing pots and pans until he died at age eighty. His legacy included no great accomplishments. He'd simply been a humble kitchen servant. But with the publication of his writings years after his death, he became recognized as one of the spiritual giants of his age. Throughout the generations since, his life has continued to be a source of inspiration and instruction.

His book, *The Practice of the Presence of God,* speaks practically about how God intended us to experience life. Brother Lawrence understood that the purpose of life is to live every moment in awareness of God's presence. Alert to God's nearness, he viewed all activity as holy. "The time of business," he wrote, "does not with me differ from the time of prayer; and in the noise and clatter of my kitchen, while several persons are at the same time calling for different things, I possess God in as great tranquility as if I were upon my knees at the Blessed Sacrament."[3]

Brother Lawrence stressed that there can be no distinction made between the secular and the sacred. The sanctity and value of work doesn't depend on the kind of work we're doing but on our personal disposition. "Our sanctification," he wrote, "does not depend upon *changing* our works, but in doing for God's sake that which we commonly do for our own good." For God, he liked to point out, "regards not the greatness of the work, but the love with which it is performed."[4]

CONTINUING THE WORK OF GOD

Work is not a nuisance to be avoided or punishment to be endured. Work is a gift given to me from the hands of a benevolent and kind God. Holiness and work are not mutually exclusive. Work is what I do to continue what God wants done. Sitting at my laptop searching for just the right words to say about work continues the work of God. Maintaining a garden that is attractive, colorful and inviting is a continuation of God's work. Building houses that provide homes for individuals and families is cocreative. This is God's design for the ongoing work of creation.

To each person God has given gifts and talents to be used for our pleasure and to meet the needs of others. For that reason there's dignity and honor imbued in every job given and accomplished by a child of God.

My father was the first to teach me about the sanctity of work. I remember, as a young boy, going with him one day to the garage where we had our car serviced. I stood on the front bumper in order to watch the mechanic as he worked on our car's engine. Near the completion of his work the mechanic brought his grease-covered hand up to scratch his nose, leaving a thick smudge on his face. Disgusted, I looked at my dad and shouted, "Yuck, I'll never be a mechanic. Greasy hands are gross!" Immediately, my dad lifted me from the bumper and took me to a private area where he explained my offense. "Son, that man is doing something very important that neither of us is able to do. He's providing a service that God gave him to pass along to us. Never say anything about a person's work suggesting it's unimportant, insignificant and, least of all, gross!"

When the mechanic's work was done, my dad let me hand the money to the mechanic. I recall my surprise at the cost to make the repair. After paying, my dad asked if there was anything I wished to say to the mechanic. Having already been coached, I was prepared to say, "Sir, thank you for getting your hands dirty so we could drive our car home. My dad told me that if I wasn't grateful, I could walk home and use the time thinking about the importance of your work." He graciously accepted my thanks, and I thankfully was given a gracious ride home.

MONEY TALKS

I grew up in a world where most people are obsessed with making the greatest amount of money with the least possible effort. Ours is a world where money speaks loudly and convincingly. Perhaps the most tragic thing that's occurred in our society is the connection made between a service rendered and its monetary value. I remember lying in bed with our son Lee, when he was much younger, having one of those surreal bedtime conversations about things in life that really matter. With eyes sparkling he declared, "Our family is really, really rich because mom's a school teacher and you tell people about God." Interested in his perception, I asked about professional athletes. Incredulously he replied, "Dad, you're just being silly! They don't get paid. It's just a game they play."

A God-shaped view of work recognizes that work is not for personal gain; work is for giving, not just for getting. Work is not merely a private enterprise somehow detached from the rest of the world. As Joan Chittister explains, "Work is not to enable me to get ahead; the purpose of work is to enable me to get more human and to make the world more just."[5]

Chittister, a member of a Benedictine community, offers this sober appraisal of the history of work:

> We have a history of serfs who worked like slaves and sweatshops that robbed people of their human dignity and basic rights. We have lived in a capitalism that bred brutal competition and unequal distribution of goods as well as inventiveness and profit. We are watching the poor get poorer even while they are working. We see the rich get richer even when they don't. And we realize that the middle class must work harder every year just to stay where they were last year. What can possibly be good about all of that? That depends on the work we do and why we're doing it.[6]

The thing for which I am most grateful is the understanding I've been led to, that work is to be done for its own sake, not because I like doing it, I feel like doing it, or because doing it will provide profits for me to enjoy. No, work has greater importance and has broader implications. God's most effective device for re-forming my life is work. Noteworthy is the fact that work is the single exercise in gift-giving that always comes back to the giver. The more I work at anything, the better I get at my work. And the better I get at my work, the better I feel about myself and the work I've done. It's the fear of failure or being good for nothing that has threatened to destroy me. But that fear has been disarmed as I continue offering the gifts God has entrusted to me.

For most of the years I served on the Young Life staff, a relational ministry dedicated to reaching disinterested adolescents, I lived in the illu-

sion that God's singular purpose was to use me to help others understand the truth about God. I gave no thought to the possibility that God
was also working in my life to continue correcting *my* mistaken ideas
and beliefs about God. One summer afternoon as I sat gazing at the four
hundred high school folks to whom I'd be speaking later that evening,
God spoke to me. "Fil, there's something I want you to realize. This isn't
just about their confusion and mistaken ideas about me. I'm intending
to use this experience to transform some of the mistaken ways you per-
sist in thinking about me too."

VOCATION, JOB, WORK . . . IS THERE ANY DIFFERENCE?

The word *vocation* comes from the Latin word for a summons or call. It's
actually rooted in the Latin word for voice. Sadly, we've secularized and
reduced the word, so now it's just another word we use for the job we
"do." Those who are wiser understand that the meaning of *vocation* runs
deeper than a job; it involves listening for a calling voice that is intent on
leading us to what is ours to do.

Unfortunately, I've never mastered the art of listening well for that calling voice. Even when I've sensed I was hearing it, I lacked the confidence
to believe that it was the calling voice of God. How can I know whose
voice it is that I'm hearing, and how can I have confidence in what it says?
How can I trust my discernment about my vocation? How do I know
what I was meant to do? How do I determine who am I meant to be?

The voice we should listen to most as we choose a vocation . . . is the
voice that we might think we should listen to least, and that is the voice
of our own gladness. What can we do that makes us the gladdest, what
can we do that leaves us with the strongest sense of sailing true north and
of peace, which is much of what gladness is? Is it making things with our
hands out of wood or stone or paint or canvas? Or is it making something we hope like truth out of words? Or is it making people laugh or
weep in a way that cleanses their spirit? I believe that if it is a thing that
makes us truly glad, then it is a good thing and it is our thing and it is

the calling voice that we were made to answer with our lives.[7]

I've grown to cherish the wisdom, freedom and hope in Buechner's words. No explanation of vocation and how to discern the calling voice's guidance has been more helpful in reshaping my understanding. Gaining this outlook about how those things I'm gifted to do and enjoy are intended to converge with those things that are good and needed has enriched my life. It's freed me from the fear of getting it all wrong and my life being a disappointment to God, others, and myself.

With hindsight's near-perfect vision, I see how often the signs of my vocation have been "hidden" in plain sight: located within the gifts and talents that are mine, the deep inner longing of my heart and awareness of the things that make me feel most alive. Twice in the past five years I've interviewed for positions that I felt would be ideal places of service. Both times another candidate was selected, leaving me devastated. However, given time's perspective, I see how terribly misguided I was by my yearning for recognition, approval and significance.

LET YOUR LIFE SPEAK

"Let your life speak" is an old Quaker saying and the title of the most wise and enduring book I've read on the subject of vocation. Yet I've often misapplied this counsel. Parker Palmer explains his misappropriation in these words: "I found those words ["Let your life speak"] encouraging, and I thought I knew what they meant: 'Let the highest truths and values guide you. Live up to those demanding standards in everything you do.'"[8]

Sounds right to me! How could I ever go wrong if I were guided by the "highest truths and values" and was faithful to "live up to those demanding standards in everything [I] did"? In fact, countless times I've chosen that path, and like Parker Palmer I found myself overwhelmed and disappointed. "The results were rarely admirable," confesses Palmer,

> often laughable, and sometimes grotesque. But always they were
> unreal, a distortion of my true self—as must be the case when one

lives from the outside in, not the inside out. I had simply found a "noble" way to live a life that was not my own, a life spent imitating heroes instead of listening to my heart.

It's always been easier to impersonate who I believed I should be than to be who I really am. At least, for a while, it's easier. Sooner or later, it becomes a huge chore. "Before you tell your life what you intend to do with it, listen for what truths and values you have decided to live up to, let your life tell you what truths you embody, what values you represent."[9]

Inside I've discovered the voice of my imposter, my false self, the person I believe I need to pretend to be if I'm to be loved. It's often misled me into believing that I'd be fulfilled if I impersonated someone rather than be myself. There's a Hasidic tale that points to the terrible fallacy in this faulty voice's counsel. Old Rabbi Zusya said, "In the coming world, they will not ask me: 'Why were you not Moses?' They will ask me: 'Why were you not Zusya?' "[10]

The most appealing and compelling lives I've encountered are those who seem content and happy with their life. I think of my father-in-law, a commercial pilot who simply loved flying; a surgeon who said, "I can't express the satisfaction and communion with God I feel when I do my work"; a friend who's cherished working in Washington, D.C., for many years, loving Jesus in the distressing disguise of the poorest of the poor, the homeless. And by the grace of God I even think of me, listening to those who offer the gift of vulnerability as they entrust their souls to me for spiritual direction. I who enjoy the honor of guiding retreats for followers of Jesus who are yearning for a deeper sense of his presence in their daily life. I who enjoy the luxury of a vocation that enhances my own awareness of God's nearness and the delight God finds in my company.

ROAD TO HEAVEN

For some, vocation becomes a "road to heaven" that's available to all. I've known many who would pay for the privilege of doing the things their vocation allows and some who in fact do pay. I heard of a Western journalist, watching Mother Teresa care for one of the dying, who couldn't help observing, "I wouldn't do that for a million dollars." To which Mother Teresa replied, "Neither would I."

My deepest calling is to be the person God created. There's no gift I have to offer that will provide God or me or those near me more pleasure, delight and good than being the me God intended. What we seek in a vocation is discovered and expressed when we engage wholeheartedly in the task that is at hand.

Years ago, with rapt attention I listened as storyteller, retreat leader and author Bob Benson offered some deeply personal and insightful reflections on the apostle Paul's words "think of what you were when you were called" (1 Corinthians 1:26). Bob began telling a simple story that at first had me wondering where he was headed.

"Early last spring I was planting my garden." Explaining that it was late in the evening and he had plans for leaving the following morning on an extended trip. He was hurrying to finish before darkness fell. Having run out of sticks and labels to mark the rows, he was about to retrieve some more when, suddenly, he wondered what the purpose was for labels anyway. By the time he returned from the trip, the plants would be up and he could see where they were growing. From prior experience he knew how to identify the plants, and the animals that typically came to feast on his garden knew the identity of the plants, and certainly the seeds knew what they were. "Who needs labels?"

Heeding this new insight, Bob simply covered the seeds with the moist earth and gently patted the beds and said, "Go ahead and sprout. You know what you are."

I have a profound sense that the voice of God is calling out in the deepest, darkest place of my soul. The great challenge and test of my faith is to trust that voice enough to heed what it's saying and thus discover who I really am and what my potential is.

Therefore, if it seems that I'm hearing nothing from the outside (where I'm accustomed to hearing), then I have only to listen to the voice that is deep inside me. That, I have come to believe, is the calling of God.

Often the problem is not having enough confidence in myself—or the time or the patience—to listen to the whispering voice. Most of the time I don't hear it. But it doesn't really matter, because in all likelihood, if I did, I wouldn't trust it. So, like most others, I search for what I'm to do in some other way. I ask for advice from friends, family members and professionals. I read books and listen to tapes. I put out fleeces, flip coins, take aptitude tests and personality inventories. Not bad things to do unless they keep me from doing the most important thing. And that is, to believe that I have the answers deep within.

Paul's simple yet profound words suggest that the calling does indeed come from within the lives of the most unlikely and "foolish." No doubt, I think I'm unlikely, but God doesn't. I have difficulty believing that God could do great things in me, but God doesn't.

If God can give a tiny seed life and help it to become what it was intended to be, why is it so unbelievably hard to believe that God can do the same for and inside me? Having clearly done this for beans and squash and tomatoes and corn, it shouldn't be too much of a stretch to believe that God's image is in me, calling me to be who I've been called to be. The trick is to listen for the voice, to hear it, to believe it and to trust it enough to act on it.

It's that easy, and it's that hard.

PART TWO

OUTWARD

7

FRIENDSHIPS

EXPERIENCING OTHERS ON THE JOURNEY

David G. Benner

According to C. S. Lewis, there are four basic human loves: affection, eros, charity and friendship. Long overshadowed by romantic love, friendship is easily undervalued, but the ancients viewed friendship as the crown of life, the fulfillment of all that is most distinctively human. Moderns all too often assess the value of friendship primarily in terms of its usefulness for achieving material ends (friends as business contacts) or minimizing boredom and loneliness (friends as people to kill time with).

The principal reason friendship is so undervalued is probably that too few people have ever experienced a significant, enduring friendship. All but the hermit have acquaintances, but typically such relationships involve no more than a passing connection. Most people also have colleagues with whom they work or associates with whom they spend regular time, but this still falls short of the ideals of friendship.

The coin of friendship has been continuously devalued by being applied to these lesser forms of relationship. Relationships between acquaintances or associates involve little of the intimacy, trust, commitment and loyalty of real friendships. Friendships may grow out of these more casual relationships but are not the same. Unfortunately, true friendships are also much more rare. Friendship is one of God's special gifts to humans. Remarkably, *friendship* is one of the terms God uses to describe the relationship he desires with us. Friendship is therefore no ordinary relationship. We cheapen it when we reduce it to mere acquaintanceship. The ideals of friendship are worth preserving.

MODEL FRIENDSHIPS

In light of the fact that friendship has its origins and foundation in the character of God, it's not surprising that the Bible is full of remarkable stories of friendship. One of the greatest examples of a spiritual friendship in the literature of the West is the biblical account of the friendship of David and Jonathan. This story begins in 1 Samuel 18:1 with the following disarmingly powerful words: "After David had finished talking with Saul, Jonathan became one in spirit with David, and he loved him as himself." Fourteen chapters later it ends with Jonathan's death and David's cry of anguish:

> I grieve for you, Jonathan my brother;
>   you were very dear to me.
>   Your love for me was wonderful,
>   more wonderful than that of women. (2 Samuel 1:26)

These words were spoken by a man who knew the love of women. Recall David's lust-filled affair with Bathsheba, an illicit love that burned so strongly that it led David to murder her husband. But he recognized that the love he shared with Jonathan—each loving the other as himself—was a unique gift of wonder. As the story of that love unfolds, we see it expressed in acts of loyalty, enormous risk taking, tender devotion and ultimately a covenant of eternal friendship sworn in the name of the Lord and binding on their descendants for all time (1 Samuel 20:42).

The Old Testament book of Ruth tells another extraordinary friendship story—actually the story of two interlocking friendships. Ruth's remarkable friendship with her mother-in-law, Naomi, forms the foundation for the story and stands as a monument to the devotion of true friends. After Ruth has lost her husband, brother-in-law and father-in-law to death, Naomi urges her to return to her homeland and find another husband. This leads Ruth to assert her love for Naomi in the following familiar words:

> Don't urge me to leave you or to turn back from you. Where you go I will go, and where you stay I will stay. Your people will be my people and your God my God. Where you die I will die, and there I will be buried. May the LORD deal with me, be it ever so severely, if anything but death separates you and me. (Ruth 1:16-17)

God honored Ruth's loyalty to her friend by introducing Boaz, a relation of her deceased husband, to the circle of friendship. What Boaz had heard of Ruth's faithfulness and kindness to her mother-in-law touched him, and he returned the gift of friendship to Ruth. This initially took the form of support and protection but eventually culminated in marriage.

The most remarkable biblical friendship story is that of Jesus and his disciples. This is particularly important for us, as it gives us a window to the relationship God claims to want with us. Not surprisingly, it also gives us one of the clearest biblical presentations of the ideals of friendship.

Jesus' relationship with his disciples begins, in each case, with his initiative. One by one, he invites them to follow him. This call was more than an invitation to belief or even to physical journeying together—it was a call to the transformational journey of Christian spirituality. Although Jesus was clear about the costs of following him, the disciples could never have fully known the implications of their responding. It would forever change them and the world.

Following Christ always has that implication. Jesus' call was to journey with him. In addition to his emphasis on the costs of discipleship, he assured his disciples that he would never leave them alone, would share the intimacy he experienced with the Father with them, and ultimately would seal his friendship by laying down his life for them. He also assured them that if they did the will of his Father in heaven, they would be to him as his mother and brothers.

Jesus was not just talk. He did not just speak of friendship; he actually offered it to his disciples and followers. He

- spent time with them—eating, drinking, walking and discussing things that were important to both him and them (Luke 24:13-45)

- shared the most painful depths of his experience with them (Matthew 26:38)

- shared insights that were not disclosed to those outside the circle of friendship (Matthew 13:36-52)

- humbled himself in offering acts of tender care (John 13:1-17)

- offered them emotional support, repeatedly assuring them that there was no need for fear and demonstrating genuine concern for their feelings (John 14)

- invited and answered their questions (Luke 9:18-27)

- related to them in ways that were loving yet challenged them to grow (John 13:1-17)

Reading the Gospels with a focus on the relationship between Jesus and the disciples is a powerful experience. Listen to Jesus' words to his disciples as you place yourself in their company:

> Greater love has no one than this, that he lay down his life for his friends. You are my friends if you do what I command. I no longer call you servants, because a servant does not know his master's business. Instead, I have called you friends, for everything that I learned from my Father I have made known to you. You did not choose me, but I chose you and appointed you to go and bear fruit—fruit that will last. Then the Father will give you whatever you ask in my name. (John 15:13-16)

These words are among the most amazing recorded in Scripture. Jesus, the Christ, the Son of God, invites us into the intimacy of the circle of friendship that exists between him and the Father. The friendship that Jesus offers he has shared from eternity within the Godhead. The Christian doctrine of the Trinity places friendship at the very heart of the nature of God. And almost unbelievably, the eternal interflow of companionship that binds Father, Son and Holy Spirit to each other extends to those Jesus calls to be his followers and friends.

IDEALS OF SPIRITUAL FRIENDSHIP

Five closely interrelated elements appear in the relationships between David and Jonathan; Ruth, Naomi and Boaz; and Jesus and his disciples. They are love, honesty, intimacy, mutuality and accompaniment. Let's look more closely at each of these ideals of spiritual friendship.

Love. Friendships involve a bond of love, never simply an obligation of love. Jonathan was described as loving David as himself and being one in spirit with him. This made his sacrifices and risks inconsequential.

True friends experience each other as being part of themselves in some profound way. Once I heard a woman describe such a friendship as involving the discovery of the other half of her soul. Plato used this same metaphor to characterize deep friendship: the experience of a single soul in two bodies.

Metaphorical allusions to being one in spirit or soul should not be interpreted so literally as to suggest that apart from such relationships we are missing half of our selves. But they do point toward the sense of deep connection that exists in friendships like David and Jonathan's. This connection involves much more than recognition of an overlap of interests or values. People can be similar in personality yet not experience any deep soul connection. They can also be different from each other yet experience a deep soul connection. Like Siamese twins connected in their bodies, soul friends are connected in the depths of their inner self.

According to C. S. Lewis, the bond of deep friendship involves the experience of another person as what he calls a "kindred soul." He suggests that kindred souls are people who see the same truth—or perhaps better, care about the same truth.[1] Friendship involves passion. In contrast to romantic love, where the passion is between the individuals, in friendship the passion is shared in relation to something outside of the friendship. Friends share a love of at least one thing—be it ideas, politics, art or the spiritual journey. Apart from this there would be nothing for the friendship to be about. As noted by Lewis, those who have nothing can share nothing; those who are going nowhere can have no fellow travelers. The sense of being a kindred soul is therefore based on shared passion regarding important aspects of life.

While friends can be lovers and lovers should ideally be friends, Lewis notes some helpful contrasts between these two forms of love, if we don't push them too far apart. Speaking metaphorically, he suggests that whereas lovers stand gazing into each other's eyes, friends walk side by side in the pursuit of their shared interests. Lovers are always talking to each other about their relationship. In contrast, friends hardly ever do so. Their focus is elsewhere—on the journey they share.

This is clear in the relationship between Jesus and the disciples. While the disciples were more than workers recruited to a cause, their focus was not just their friendship with Jesus. Jesus continually pointed them toward the will of the Father and the kingdom activities that were part of surrender to his will. Their friendship was not simply a feel-good mutual admiration society. It was built around knowing, loving and serving God.

Another important difference between friends and lovers is that friendship is much less vulnerable to jealousy. In contrast to romantic love, friends lose nothing by sharing their friends with others. There should be no place for exclusiveness in friendship. In fact, under normal circumstances, circles of friendship expand as other "kindred souls" are discovered, each addition to the circle enhancing, not diluting, the value of the network of relationships. Each person in the circle of friendship brings out particular aspects of the personality of each of the others. Each can thus be welcomed rather than warded off as a threat.

The inclusiveness of Jesus' friendship must have been difficult for the disciples to understand. They were used to friendships that were more exclusive, where the boundaries between inner and outer circles of acquaintances were clearer. Imagine their shock when after reprimanding the unknown man who was casting out demons, Jesus pronounced all who were not against him as for him (Mark 9:38-40). Imagine their shock when he welcomed sinners and outcasts into his circle of friendship. Imagine their shock when women were publicly included.

Friends show their love in an endless variety of ways. Undergirding these, however, is a central desire for the blessing of the other person. Friends long for each other's well-being and do whatever they can to support it.

In caring for me, my friends support my emotional, spiritual, intellectual and physical development. They do not simply want me to stay as I am. Rather, they seek my growth. They want me to become all I can be. They want me to develop my gifts and fulfill my potential. They want nothing less for me than that I become the full-orbed person I am called from eternity to be in Christ. They want nothing less than my wholeness and holiness. What a blessing it is to have even one such friendship!

It is important to note that friendship love is grounded in reality. This begins with the absence of idealization. The great weakness of romantic love is that lovers see each other through the unrealistic lens of idealization. This is, of course, why romantic love is unstable. Eventually reality always sets in and shatters the unrealistic perceptions of the loved one.

True friends, in contrast, see each other realistically. Because they know each other so well, they know the weaknesses that are hidden from the view of those at a distance. This awareness, however, does not diminish the respect, affection and admiration that they feel. But they are not prone to idolization. Friends are not fascinated by each other. Nor are they awestruck. They know each other not by the outer garb of persona but by the dependable and relatively stable elements of habit, character, disposition and trait. It is this down-to-earth quality of friendships that gives them stability and endurance. They may be unromantic, but they are anchored in reality.

One incident in the Gospel record of interactions between Jesus and his disciples is particularly striking in this regard. Matthew tells the story of how Jesus called him to disciple friendship, leaving his previous work as a tax collector. Tax collectors in first-century Palestine were notoriously corrupt and almost universally despised. So when Jesus went to Matthew's house for dinner and some of Matthew's fellow tax collectors turned up to meet his new friend, the Pharisees criticized Jesus for eating and drinking with sinners. His response is instructive. Rather than defend Matthew and his friends, Jesus accepted their status as sinners. In fact he went further, identifying with them and declaring that it was sinners who were his priority and not the righteous, as it's the sick, not the healthy, who need a doctor (Matthew 9:10-13).

Such grounding in reality gives true friendships their enormous growth potential. Anything that calls a person to a firmer grasp on reality calls him or her to growth. There is no meaningful growth apart from solid reality contact.

One final aspect of friendship love that should be noted is loyalty. Jonathan's loyalty to David is at the core of the story's timeless appeal. The same is true of Ruth's loyalty to Naomi. Loyalty is always a gift of love. It is a gift, as it cannot be demanded. However, without it there is no real friendship—certainly nothing deserving to be called a spiritual friendship. Loyalty is given to the friend as an act of honor for the friendship and the friend.

Loyalty means faithfulness to commitments, spoken and unspoken. True friends preserve confidentiality, commit themselves to being honest with each other, avoid public criticism of each other and offer each other courtesy and respect. They carry their friends' best interests with them, always seeking to protect and advance them. They are also prepared to protect those interests, even at personal cost. Loyalty sometimes requires a sacrifice of self-interest. But this is a small price to pay for the priceless pearl of friendship.

Honesty. Because friends desire each other's growth and development, love demands honesty. It confronts illusions and dares to risk temporary discomfort by calling us to the truth. Jesus' love for the disciples meant that he could not ignore some of the things he saw in them. When he predicted Peter's denial, he wasn't showing off his prophetic abilities; he was confronting Peter's pride. When he rebuked the disciples for their lack of trust in his ability to take care of them during a storm at sea, it was to encourage faith. And when he heard them arguing about which of them was greatest, his confrontation was motivated by desire for their spiritual well-being.

One particularly striking example of speaking the truth in love comes in the encounter between Jesus and Peter after Jesus' prediction of his own death. Peter protested, and Jesus spoke to him words that must have felt unusually harsh: "Get behind me, Satan! . . . You do not have in mind the things of God, but the things of men" (Mark 8:33). Did these words reflect a lack of care, or did they rather reflect deep love? Obviously the real lack of care would have been to overlook the triumphalistic assumptions that were lurking behind Peter's protest. It was love that motivated Jesus to confront Peter.

Love cannot ignore things that are self-destructive in the loved one. By daring to be honest with us, friends offer us invaluable opportunities for growth. They can help us penetrate our self-deceptions and cherished illusions. Just as the retina of the human eye contains a blind spot, so too the human soul contains a blind spot. Soul friends help us see things we can't see on our own. There are things about ourselves that we would never recognize without them. The true soul friend will not accept our self-deceptions but will gently and firmly confront us with our soul blindness. Soul friends want each other to settle for nothing short of becoming the whole and holy person they are called to be.

When I reflect on how over the years my own friends have challenged me to grow, I recall numerous examples. Most of them relate to the personality thread that is my particular besetting sin. One good friend in high school confronted me on my arrogance. I deflected the confrontation. However, I took more note of it when another friend a few years later framed the same issue in terms of my detachment. Some years later my closest friend—my wife—prodded me to reflect on the anger that often seemed to lurk beneath the surface.

A pattern emerged, built around the dynamics of pride, detachment and feelings of entitlement. These dynamics are right at the center of the blind spot of my soul. They are sins I could not possibly see apart from the gentle confrontation of my friends. While I was usually less open than I should have been to what these good friends offered me at the point of each confrontation, I owe them all an enormous debt of gratitude. My struggle in these areas continues. However, I would be at a much worse place than I am were it not for friends who have dared to offer loving nudges to growth. Nudges are never enough to ensure a response. They do, however, provide an opportunity.

When friends confront each other in these ways, they do so in love. This increases enormously the probability that the interaction will produce growth. If I suspect that my friend is merely attacking me, it's easy to ignore his or her challenge. However, when it's clear that my friend is pushing me simply because he loves me and wants me to grow, the confrontation is much harder to ignore.

The challenge is communicating love through a critical balance of support and confrontation. Confrontation without support will never be experienced as love. But support without confrontation will always remain an insipid form of love. Friends communicate their love by offering emotional and spiritual support. This includes support for their friends' growth. However, that support will never be contingent on growth— withdrawn if I fail to make sufficiently good use of it.

Finally, honesty is not just something that friends try to practice. It is also something they delight in experiencing. The honesty that characterizes genuine and deep friendships is not just the honesty of words. It is also the honesty of being. Friends feel sufficiently safe with each other that they can relax and be what they are. Since I am already known and loved for who I am, pretensions can be set aside and I can be myself. Ralph Waldo Emerson describes a friend as a person with whom I can think aloud. This freedom from a need to manage appearances is a fundamental and basic component of all true friendships.

Intimacy. When people long for friendships that are more meaningful, they want someone with whom they can be known with the freedom and honesty I have just described. And they want to know the other person in the same deep ways. In short, they want intimacy. Jesus' offer of friendship is an offer of intimacy. He wants to share our lives and share our experience. More remarkably, he invites us to share his life and his experience.

Consider how astounding it was that Jesus shared his anguish in the garden of Gethsemane with the disciples (Matthew 26:36-46). First, note that he didn't go to the garden alone. We might assume that his friendship with his Father would have been enough and that he would simply share his feelings with him in prayer. But no, he took three of his disciples when he went to this garden to deal with what he knew to be his imminent arrest and crucifixion. Listen, then, to what he shared with them in the garden. The honesty and intimacy of the conversation is remarkable. He told them that his soul was bursting within him, overwhelmed with sorrow. And he told them he was close to not being able to take it any longer; he was at the point of death. Then he asked them to keep watch with him—to share his experience.

Intimacy is shared experience. Jesus shared his experience with those who were his closest friends. And he invited them to accompany him as he walked through this experience. Intimacy can be experienced in a variety of forms. Two people are vocationally intimate when they share work experiences, recreationally intimate when they share experiences of play, intellectually intimate when they share intellectual experiences, emotionally intimate when they share emotional experiences, and spiritually intimate when they share spiritual experiences.

Spheres of intimacy reinforce each other. Friends who share intellectual discoveries become more deeply engaged with each other, for example, if they also share experiences that are political, spiritual or aesthetic. Dynamic spiritual friendships yearn for shared experience in a growing number of areas of life.

Like many other forms of relationship, friendships tend not to remain static. They evolve or devolve—grow or shrink. If a friendship deepens over time, intimacy increases in depth and breadth. In fact, growth in intimacy is one of the best measures of growth in a friendship. In contrast, a sure sign of a dying friendship is a decrease of intimacy.

Spiritual friends share with each other at the level of their soul. This doesn't mean that they talk about only serious, personal or spiritual matters. However, if they never share at this level, the relationship is not worthy of being called a spiritual—or soul—friendship. *Soul* refers to the whole person, with particular attention to one's inner life. Soul intimacy therefore is built on sharing the inner self. Sharing at the level of their souls means that friends' intimacy is not restricted to experiences with the external world.

Friends who enjoy soul intimacy never settle for gossip or simple information exchange. Instead they use the data of events as springboards for the sharing of feelings, perceptions, values, ideas and opinions. The conversations of such friends are never merely about what happened in their lives or the world but move from this to how they experience, react to and understand what happened. Dialogue continually moves from the surface to the depths, from the external to the internal. This is the crucial distinctive of dialogue in spiritual friendships.

Spiritual intimacy demands this attentiveness to the inner world. Soul conversations invite inclusion of the spiritual dimension of life when they pay attention to inner experience, not simply the external world. Our spirituality is most clearly expressed in the deep longings that enliven us. Longings, in contrast to mere desires, come from our depths. Longings reflect spirit bubbling up to the surface—what we might theologically describe as a response of spirit to Spirit. Attending to the spiritual is attending to these stirrings in our depths.

Spiritual intimacy involves sharing these longings. It also involves sharing other aspects of inner experience neglected in more superficial exchanges—anxieties, hopes, concerns, dreams (both metaphorical and literal), preoccupations and ruminations. Things that might be counted as trivial are valued and shared because of this attentiveness to the inner world.

Most important, however, spiritual intimacy involves sharing our experience of God. I might tell my friend about a recent period of spiritual dryness in which God seemed absent. Or I might express gratitude associated with an answer to prayer. Or I might share an unusually strong sense of spiritual hunger. This is not the same as discussing theology, church politics or even the Sunday sermon. Genuine spiritual intimacy involves sharing my experience, not simply my ideas. One component of this shared experience will usually be my experience of God.

The intimacy that exists between spiritual friends is a togetherness that honors separateness. I must never view my friend as an extension of myself—my property, my possession or someone who exists for me. This is the basis of the nonpossessiveness that should characterize spiritual friendships. Without an honoring of the separateness of each person, the intimacy of friendship is destructively symbiotic.

Honoring separateness removes some of the obligation that exists in other relationships. Friends owe nothing to each other except love. They are separate, autonomous people. Children and parents each owe the other a great number of things. Similarly, core obligations define the marital relationship. Friends have fewer formal obligations. Apart from love, they owe each other nothing. If they give more than they owe, this is a gift of grace.

Possessiveness always betrays a destructive dynamic in any relationship. The fruit of possessiveness is jealousy. Jealousy is as destructive in friendship as it is in marriage. Possessiveness, and the related dynamics of control and manipulation, always reflects an absence of respect for the separateness and autonomy of the other person.

It is important to remember that even the most intimate friendship can't eliminate the strangeness that exists between any two people. The friend always remains partly stranger. It is naive to assume that two people can ever know each other completely. Real friendships acknowledge the mystery of the other person—a mystery that can at times delight and at other times disappoint. But it is this strangeness, this separateness, that keeps passion alive in a friendship.

Space always nourishes genuine friendship. A healthy friendship thus honors the space in the relationship. Each gives the other lots of room for friends, interests and experiences that form no part of the shared experience of the friendship. Such separateness is based on the awareness that my friend's life is not my life. His journey may connect to mine in some important ways, but because he is separate from me, his calling and journey are his own. As noted by Thomas Moore, "The soul . . . needs flight as much as it needs embrace."[2] Although we walk side by side, and at times hand in hand, we walk two separate and distinct paths. True friends never lose sight of this fact.

Mutuality. One important difference between friendship and other relationships of care is the presence of some degree of mutuality. I can offer support, counseling or ministry to someone who doesn't offer anything in exchange, but I can be a friend only to someone who offers the same in return. Friends offer each other what they receive from each other. This reciprocal nature of friendship marks it as distinct from all other relationships of care.

The mutuality that was present in Jesus' friendship with his disciples is truly remarkable. He didn't invite them only to be followers but to be friends. And beyond this, he didn't just offer to be their friend but invited them to be his. Recognizing that friendships are supposed to be mutual and reciprocal, we feel betrayed and used when they aren't. We complain when we are always on the giving end of a friendship, never on the receiving end. Such a relationship may have depth and significance and may be worthy of being called a relationship of soul care. But we set ourselves up for frustration when we view it as a friendship, for then we expect mutuality. It would be much better to view it as a relationship of ministry or service, in which I give care but don't expect any in return.

Viewing everyone to whom I extend Christian charity as a friend dilutes the concept of friendship. Similarly, viewing all relationships of pastoral care or Christian nurture as friendships introduces an element of dishonesty. Mutuality, at least at the levels experienced and expected by friends, does not form a part of most relationships of Christian ministry.

The mutuality of a friendship is based on a rhythm in which the giving and the receiving of each will balance over time, not within a given day or week or even month. But friendships aren't primarily relationships of care. Primarily they are relationships of soul intimacy. Friends care for each other when this is needed, but that caring isn't the only dimension of the relationship. If it becomes so, if the mutuality is lost and the shared exploration of the world that was originally motivated by being kindred spirits is missing, the relationship has shifted from a soul friendship to something else.

Mutuality does not mean equality. What Jesus offered the disciples was different from what the disciples offered Jesus. He was the spiritual teacher, they were the students. And yet he called them his friends. It was a relationship of intimacy and mutuality, even if it wasn't a relationship of equality.

Accompaniment. This brings us to the final ideal of friendship. Friends accompany each other on the journey of life. The term *accompaniment* may have musical associations for you. These associations are actually quite relevant. One of my musician friends is an accompanist for recitalists. He tells me that the challenge the musical accompanist faces is not to lead or get in the road but to stay in close supportive contact with the person he is accompanying. The challenges in spiritual accompaniment are similar.

The first interactions between Jesus and his disciples recorded in Scripture were his invitations to join him on his journey. The wonderful thing about accepting this invitation was that he then accompanied them on *their* journeys. And so it is with us. As Christ followers we participate in his life, but he also participates in ours. This is what true friends do. They accompany each other on life's journey.

Sometimes we are blessed with a friend who accompanies us for the whole of our adult life. Ruth and Naomi were blessed to be able to remain together, and one suspects that their friendship continued even after Ruth's marriage to Boaz. At other times the period of accompaniment is shorter. David and Jonathan journeyed together for only a small portion of David's life. But for however long they share friendship, true friends share enough of their separate journeys that these journeys become intertwined. Something that was separate becomes connected. My journey becomes our journey, and I am no longer alone.

Friends accompany each other by taking an active interest in each other's journey. As noted previously, this places a particular priority on the inner dimensions of that journey. But because the soul is the whole person, friends are also interested in the external aspects of each other's lives. Job frustrations, relationships with family members and other circumstances of life are shared and embraced with interest because true friends care for each other in their totality.

Because the accompaniment soul friends offer each other gives priority to the journey of the inner self, they can withstand physical separation. Even across the distance of times apart, friends can stay attuned to each other and continue to sense the flow of each other's lives. Catching up occurs quickly, and the connection seems never to have been interrupted. Accompaniment doesn't require a great deal of actual time together.

The lives of friends intermingle, and the intimacy they experience often spreads across a number of spheres of experience. They become an important part of each other's story because they share in important ways in each other's life. That sharing forms an important strand in the cord of accompaniment that binds their lives together.

GROWING TOGETHER

The ultimate test of a spiritual friendship is whether all parties are growing as a result of it. Intimate relationships can be either soul-destroying or soul-nurturing. Soul-nurturing friendships include increasing levels of

- attunement to the Spirit, hunger for God and surrender to his will
- love for others
- self-understanding and attentiveness to the voices of your inner world
- curiosity about God's creation
- enjoyment of life
- discernment of your unique self-in-Christ
- courage to follow your calling
- depth of passion and compassion
- sense of gratitude
- overall experience of holiness and wholeness

However, since none of us exists in only a single relationship, another question to be asked of any friendship is what its impact is on other relationships. For the Christian this includes our relationship with God. Every relationship we experience, particularly every significant relationship, changes us in important ways. The question is, do those changes aid our growth or hinder it? Is the overall impact of the relationship on my spiritual journey positive or negative? The possibility for both exists.

Out of a fear of the potential adverse effect on their spiritual life, some Christians avoid soul intimacy with non-Christians. Others avoid it simply because they believe it isn't possible to meet people in places of soul intimacy apart from a shared-faith journey. Both understandings are, from my point of view, tragically incorrect.

While the most intimate forms of spiritual friendship described in this chapter are restricted to those on a similar spiritual journey, there is no question that our shared humanity allows us to experience deep soul connections with others. All that is required is that we meet in places of depth, honesty and mutual respect.

I have seen wonderful friendships flourish when a Christian accepts a non-Christian partner as he is and seeks to build soul intimacy. This will never happen quickly. In fact, depending on the history of the relationship, initial overtures may be rejected and mistrusted. But soul hospitality can transform a relationship. And it can transform both parties to the relationship. It must, however, be offered as an invitation, not a strategy of manipulation. And invitations can be rejected. They carry no guarantees.

GRACE AND THE SPACE BETWEEN IDEALS AND REALITY

The ideals of friendship should not be confused with reality. In the real world friends fail each other, seek to control each other, feel possessiveness and jealousy, experience limitations in their love, and lack courage for honesty and intimacy.

The failures in the inner circle of Jesus' friends were spectacular. In spite of his best intentions and resolve, Peter denied Christ. Fear was stronger than loyalty. And Judas, whom Jesus called "friend" even at the moment when he came to betray him, was anything but a true friend.

When I think of my own closest friendships, I realize how far short of the just-discussed ideals I routinely fall. My love is limited by my inability to set aside self-interest, my honesty by my abundant and endlessly creative self-deceptions, my intimacy by my fear, genuine dialogue by my egocentricity and respect for separateness by my need to control.

But true friendships don't demand perfection. We come to them as we are and are received with grace by someone who accepts and loves the imperfect self we bring. There is, after all, no other self we can bring. Either our friend accepts us as we are, or we are forced to do the same posturing that characterizes our other relationships. The great gift of genuine friendship is that it allows us to live in the space between ideals and reality.

REFLECTING ON THE IDEALS OF SPIRITUAL FRIENDSHIP

This chapter began with a review of several biblical examples of friendship. But friendship is even more central to the Bible than these examples might suggest. Friendship has its origin and meaning in the intimacy of the eternal circle of friendship that exists within the Godhead.

If God did not experience eternal friendship within the Trinity, we would never have known the possibility of this gift of soul intimacy. Remarkably, it is this friendship that God invites us to join. This friendship forms the prototype for all human friendships.

Reflect on the friendship that has been shared from eternity between God the Father, God the Son and God the Holy Spirit. Now allow yourself to imagine the day that God decided to create humans and to invite them into this circle of friendship. As you meditate on this, allow yourself to respond to God in prayer with gratitude. How does recognizing this source of human friendship change your understanding of the ideals of friendship? Spiritual friends participate in the divinely inspired pattern of intimacy by sharing themselves and their experience. Spheres of intimacy reinforce each other and tend to either expand or contract.

Think about your closest male friendship and identify the spheres of intimacy you experience (spiritual, intellectual, aesthetic, recreational, vocational and so on). How has the nature of your intimacy changed over the past year? What challenges and opportunities do you see in this relationship?

Reflect on the spiritual intimacy you experience in your most important friendships. Do these friendships offer you a place to share regularly the stirrings of your soul? How well do you create a space where others are encouraged to share their inner journey? What makes it difficult for you to help others move from a focus on the external world to a focus on their inner experience? Of course friendships don't always live up to the ideals. Tragically, the actual experience of friendship often leads to disillusionment and disappointment.

Reflect on significant friendship failures you have experienced. What have you learned about yourself from these experiences? How have they influenced the way you approach friendships now? If your enthusiasm for spiritual friendship needs bolstering, meditate on the biblical examples of friendship listed earlier in the chapter.

If you are blessed to have one or more genuine spiritual friendships, be sure to thank God, because such friendships are not an entitlement but a gift. Christ, who said to his disciples, "You have not chosen me, but I have chosen you," might say of Christian friends, "You have not chosen each other, but I have chosen you for each other."

Spiritual friendship is not a reward for good behavior. It is the means by which God reveals his goodness by helping us know others and ourselves and thereby know him. It is a gift God gives to us. It is a gift we can give to others.

8

SEX

LEARNING TO TELL YOUR SEXUAL STORY

John D. Pierce

Perhaps you are like me. When I skim the contents page of a book about men's issues and see a chapter on the topic of sex, I turn there first. Call it curiosity, but I wonder what tack the author will take with this big topic and if there will be anything new. If you turned here first, then you are in good company.

If you want men's attention, just use that simple three letter word—S-E-X. Our culture can associate almost anything with sex, and with good reason. Our sexual experiences have produced some of the most powerful feelings we will know—from exquisite pleasure or pain to excited anticipation or dread to restoring release or recoil. You get the picture, right? Our sexuality is woven deeply into our fabric. Therefore it is not much of a jump to see that our sexual story as men can be a central place where God invites us in to the transformational journey.

It's late, but my body is awake and so is my mind. Here in the quiet darkness you'd think she could hear the cogs turning in my head, but she sleeps. I wish she knew how much I want her, or is it need her? I don't know. Want? Need? Desire? Who knows, but what I do know is that I ache inside and want some relief, but would I be loving her or loving me

*in grasping for physical relief? Am I lonely and hungry for some atten-
tion from the one who knows me best, or do I just want a break? I just
wish she were awake, wanting me as much as I want her! Why doesn't
she read my mind more often? And why does she think about it so much
less than I do; maybe that isn't true, maybe she does think about it, but
the problem is me. No, scratch that! This is crazy! You trust her and love
her and she loves you. Wake her, ask her. No! Touch her, and surely she
will rouse and get the message. No! She is exhausted and rightfully so.
. . . Father, help me rest this restlessness in me.*

SEX AND TRANSFORMATION

It takes only a moment of reflection to realize that the whirling sexual
hungers, thoughts, images and practices of men uncover the issues of the
heart. Our deepest longings to be admired, wanted, respected and loved
are revealed in our sex lives. Also exposed are our greatest battles with
foolishness, ill motives and sin. Sex can be legitimately looked at as a
loving expression of intimate union, or it can illegitimately compensate
for our real or imagined inadequacies and fears. Our sexual pursuits or
evasions uncover the mix and mire that is intertwined in our heart, revealing selfishness and demands or the honorable desires to be sacrificial
and loving. The Scriptures give us great clarity about many sexual dos
and don'ts, but there are few simple answers for the myriad of sexual
questions many of us would face if our own sexual dramas were put under the microscope.

THORNS AND TRANSFORMATION

"Three times I pleaded with the Lord to take it away from me. But he said
to me, 'My grace is sufficient for you, for my power is made perfect in
weakness.' Therefore I will boast all the more gladly about my weaknesses, so that Christ's power may rest on me" (2 Corinthians 12:8-9).

I never get to choose my thorns. Scripture seems to indicate that Paul
didn't get to choose his either. You know what I mean by *thorns*, don't

you; those purposeful things that for whatever reason God allows to happen in our lives for distinct periods of times or even for life? Scholars have speculated a great deal about what the thorn was that the apostle Paul prayed to have removed. Many think it was related to his sight. Whatever it was, from the sound of things Paul's life worked pretty well for him until he encountered Jesus.

It wasn't until his encounter with the Lord on the road to Damascus that Paul's life took a major turn (Acts 9). He went from being a greatly re-spected Pharisee wielding great intelligence, power and influence to being blinded by God and led around by the hand. He was at the mercy of Jesus, who just moments before his blinding was his greatest enemy. This expe-rience could perhaps be called the birth place of Paul's transformation. Needless to say, it was an incredible challenge to his way of seeing life.

Although his sight was eventually restored, Scripture hints that he continued to struggle with his eyesight. Even after years of faithful ser-vice to Christ—through receiving lashes; being beaten with rods and stoned and shipwrecked; in danger from rivers, bandits, his own coun-trymen and false brothers; constantly on the move; laboring and toiling; going without sleep and food; and being cold and naked (see 2 Corin-thians 11:23-28)—God still allowed the thorn to remain. Why? Paul tells us the thorn was purposefully left unchanged to keep him from be-coming conceited (2 Corinthians 12:7). Paul made peace with his thorn and, more importantly, with God.

I have spent many years trying to make sense of and asking God to release me from my thorns. *Why did God leave me with these limitations?* I wondered. But I have finally come to the place where I am convinced he made no mistakes with me. I now understand my thorns to be my allies and his blessing on me. He has redeemed my story many times over and transformed my perspective. I didn't choose my thorns, but I did get to choose how I respond to them.

I am not where I use to be, thankfully. Like Paul, I too have made peace with my thorns and with God. While perfection is nowhere in sight, I have a growing appreciation for what lies ahead. My process started with a deeper look into my sexual story. God weaves his thread into every aspect of our stories, and our sexual stories are no exception.

SEXUAL STORIES MATTER

"We should not be ashamed to discuss what God was not ashamed to create."[1]

Have you ever told someone your sexual story? No, I don't mean some lewd recounting of your conquests or some meaningless revisiting of all your failures. Rather, have you ever thought about or told your sexual story to discern the issues of your own heart that impede your development as God's man? If you have never risked being open in this area, sharing with a trusted friend, then it is possible that this aspect of your life is inhibiting your spiritual formation.

Many of us who have experienced God's unlimited kindness through Christ have sex lives that are closed off to God and others. God is allowed to influence our friendships, marriages and futures, but our sexuality is buttressed against Godly influence, frank discussion or the fresh air of bigger perspectives. Inundated daily with messages that encourage us to go for the gusto, we are easily led to make sexual happiness our goal. Our culture asks, Why wait for marriage? And if you are married, why wait for your wife? Our junk e-mail extols the possibilities of sexual pleasures. It's just a click away. Fantasy meetings in Internet chat rooms or regular dates with pornography (and masturbation) are an alluring diversion to loneliness, difficult marriages, anger and stress. We need to tell our stories to give God access to the sealed areas of our lives that need his presence most.

When I first breached the silence that shrouded my sexual story, I had the distinct feeling that I was breaking the seal on an airtight room that had long been locked off to light and fresh air. I had no sense as to how my maturity had been impeded by my sexual wounds and sin. As a young man I vaguely knew that I didn't measure up to God's standards because I was more often than not disobedient in my sexual desires, thought and behaviors. And in my naive understanding of his view toward me, I believed God wanted flawlessness from me rather than what a good father would want for his son—progress toward maturity. As the light flooded in, I began to see from a new perspective.

WE ALL HAVE SEXUAL STORIES: WHICH DO WE TELL?

A man's sexual development generally progresses in similar fashion from guy to guy—awareness, exploration, experimenting, pursuing, relating, committing and maturing. I offer some of my sexual story as an example.

As a child I became aware that girls are quite different than boys in their physical features. I remember playing doctor and spin the bottle, and in those early experiences I learned that girls and boys are not alike in some very important ways. Elementary school brought crushes. Nell was a neighborhood girl. I was licked by puppy love, but she never knew.

In early adolescence I talked about sex with friends. As only adolescent boys can, we speculated about which girls would do what and how far they had gone around the bases. I learned how to objectify girls and viewed them as mere "bases" or body parts. I used all the cussing, slang and bravado I could muster to buffet against the mystery, fear and intrigue of being a man with a girl. I got my sex education through pornography; it taught me how "it" was supposed to be and how I was supposed to be—or so I thought. I fondled, or should I say fumbled, a couple of girls behind the movie theater. I learned about fantasy and how my mind could go places I knew I never could or should. I found masturbation early, and its practice absorbed my attention.

In late adolescence I tried the "going together" thing with girls my age; it usually didn't go to well, but I never told anyone. I dated for a month or two in high school—I guess you would call it that. I often howled at the moon, longing to matter to some desirable girl who would have never considered me. I "scored" sexually (as the guys called it back then) and fell hopelessly into infatuation. I called it love; she called it a drunken mistake. Feelings of rejection visited and stayed.

In college I learned about long-term dating, breaking up and commitment. I had become a believer, and sex with others was now off-limits, but adolescent thinking and behavior remained in the recesses of my mind.

Years after college, I found my bride and impulsively asked for her hand under a romantic full moon by the sea; and then hours later I backed out. Months later, I vowed to her again; luckily she had waited. My commitment stuck. We explored each other emotionally, physically, relationally. We married. We "made love" and broke the bed. We had children. In the ups and downs of our sixteen years of marriage, we have engaged in the art of loving, passionate and fun sexual union. We have learned a lot—and here we are.

On the exterior I am like many of you. Together, we could have a great conversation about the transforming work God has done and still needs to do in my sex life. But if I were honest, there's a lot missing in the story above, and my contention is that it's in the missing stuff that the deepest questions and issues of the heart reside.

STORIES DOWN UNDER

The underside of my sexual story is significantly different from the story above. Beyond a quick glance, a penetrating look exposes a different reality that exists for us all to varying degrees. There is a big difference between being safe (how we spin our story for presentation and acceptability) and the authentic truth of what we think and feel on the inside. For many years what I felt on the inside was very different from what I portrayed on the outside. The term for this is *duplicity,* hiding the full truth by presenting what I believe is acceptably true. Some call it pretending, some call it lying, others call it surviving. All can be true. The fact is, though, in order for real growth to happen, our walls of duplicity must be taken down so the light of God's truth can penetrate the places in us that still live in fear and indignity.

For years my inside sexual story was hidden behind the walls of addictive behaviors, denial, competence, niceness, tough talk and lies. I was committed to keeping my true sexual story to myself because I was convinced that I would experience immeasurable loss if I ever got honest. At the age of seventeen, after I turned to Christ as Lord, I pursued honesty in many areas of my life, but my real sexual struggles were not in the equation.

SEXUAL DISTORTIONS AND QUESTIONS OF THE HEART

During the first seventeen years of my life I formed, like many of you, some distorted conceptions about what would make me happy, where I belonged and what gifts I had to offer to the world. I remember questioning God. I wrestled with him about why I was saddled with my particular passions and compulsions, and not the more run of the mill ones like irresistibility, fame and fortune. A few scenes portray the distortions in my sex life and the questions that I asked God. I encourage you to ponder the distortions and questions in your heart.

Sexual exposure and shame. Sexual activity began early for me. I have many recollections, starting with being touched inappropriately in preschool. I grew up during a time when kids often played outside all day and came home when the dinner bell rang. With lots of unsupervised time, I was vulnerable to many sexual experiences. I can still recall a mortifying moment around age seven when some neighborhood friends and I were caught in a basement crawl space nakedly exploring our "equipment." "What are you doing?" came the hesitant voice of my mom. Not until that unexpected moment did the hot feeling of shame wash over me, and innocent exploration did not feel so innocent anymore. "Get dressed and send your friends home," she said. We hurriedly complied and listened in silence to her steps on the stairs.

When I came back upstairs, I waited for more to be said, but nothing was ever mentioned again. I don't say this to lay any blame, because I am not sure any parent knows best how to handle that moment. Yet the silence spoke loudly to me, and I determined in my child's mind that what we were doing was *really* wrong.

The many experiences of shame in my sexual development caused me to wonder why I had to struggle with my sexuality. I wondered why fantasies and desires flooded my young mind. Pornography, fantasy and masturbation became a daily practice that increased my feelings of guilt, shame and defectiveness. The more I was absorbed by my private thoughts, the more my feelings of isolation grew. In my best thinking I couldn't figure out how to bridge the divide between fantasy and the real relationships I longed to have. The critic in me asked regularly, *What is wrong with you?*

The power of rejection. Whoever thought it was a good thing for junior high boys to take showers together after gym certainly didn't have my best interest in mind. I can still feel the dread that came from anticipating encounters with Toby. He was the voice of torment in my adolescence. He was a natural jock; I was the underdog, and he made sure I and everyone else knew it. He ran faster, spoke louder, won more fights and caught more balls than anyone. Though I outweighed him by over a hundred pounds and overshadowed him in height, I regularly found myself speechless before his jeers. And it was in the showers that he found his greatest pleasure in ridiculing me and pushing for fights. I tried to avoid him, but he inevitably found me, and for years it was his degrading voice that filled my heart with shame.

Apart from the rejection of God, there are two significant rejections that can stunt a man's emotional, social and sexual growth. One is for a man's pursuit to be rebuffed by a woman. The second is to be deemed unworthy to stand in the company of other men. Unfortunately, I had more experiences with both kinds of rejection than I wish to recount, so I questioned my masculinity and adequacy as a man. I asked why my body betrayed me among men. I wondered why I was only a friend of beautiful girls rather than someone they desired sexually. Why wasn't I more desirable when it mattered most, and why didn't I have a present father or at least a brother my age. Feeling alone in the company of men and undesirable (at least in the way I wanted to be desired) among women left my masculinity on shaky ground.

Turning on yourself. Comparisons kill, especially when you can see the giftedness of everyone but yourself. A message that haunted me from early on was the tag that I was "sensitive" and quite frequently, being much younger than my siblings, I was tagged "too sensitive." From my earliest recollections, I not only felt things deeply but somehow too deeply. Feelings are dangerous things, you know, especially when they regularly don't match what you see in those around you. I saw things, discerned things and was aware of things that were odd to others, and so I learned early that my gifts were a setup for more pain.

The questions raged. *Why, God, did you create in me a heart that's too sensitive? Do I have to live with this lonely ache? Why was I designed this way?* I tried to numb the pain a thousand different ways. Food. Drugs. Alcohol. Fantasy. Music. Nothing filled the void I felt. So the questions continued. *Why give me the ability to see the way I do? Why give me a heart that cares and feels too much? Why do things matter too much to me? Why not give me a heart that is blind to meaning and meaninglessness, unfeeling to the hurt of others, and unfettered by the notion that my life matters?* Through these burdensome questions I was unknowingly raging against God. My shame and guilt and doubt manifested themselves in feelings of fear and humiliation, shoving me into the ever-diminishing cage of self-absorption.

The burden of fear. The questions beneath the surface of my life remained sealed in my heart. I was committed to keeping my secrets secret because I was afraid. Fear, in its worst sense, is the language of evil; it oppresses and suffocates. I was sure that had I talked about any of these things I would have been labeled and rejected. Distrust of friends, family and faith community was justified because they would not understand, so why try? But I learned early that secrets have a painful price that the keeper bears in loneliness and fear.

A pattern of descent. Isolation is dangerous. Anyone familiar with war

knows the way to win is to divide and conquer. I was at war with myself.
I believed that my thoughts, my attitudes, my behaviors and my heart
were all wrong (and much of it was), but the most painful thing was the
belief that I was wrong! Dedicated to never allowing my real self to be
seen, I could not see myself in a balanced way. I knew what went on in
my head and heart, and it didn't seem to match the sexual stories of so
many I thought I knew. I was convinced there wasn't a place safe or good
enough to be honest about what was in me. My shame begat more
shame, and my self-loathing only increased my despair. Brennan Manning describes my pattern of descent well:

> Wallowing in shame, remorse, self-hatred, and guilt over real or
> imagined failings in our past lives betrays a distrust in the love of
> God. It shows that we have not accepted the acceptance of Jesus
> Christ and thus have rejected the total sufficiency of his redeeming
> work. Preoccupation with our past sins, present weaknesses, and
> character defects gets our emotions churning in self-destructive
> ways, closes us within the mighty citadel of self, and preempts the
> presence of a compassionate God. From personal experience I can
> testify that the language of low self-esteem is harsh and demand-
> ing; it abuses, accuses, criticizes, rejects, finds fault, blames, con-
> demns, reproaches, and scolds in a monologue of impatience and
> chastisement.[2]

Fortunately, my self-conceptions and preoccupying questions have
changed significantly because of the kindness, understanding and patient provision of God. He knew what I didn't.

HOPING IN THE GOD OF THE UPSIDE DOWN

"There was given me a thorn in my flesh, a messenger of Satan, to torment me" (2 Corinthians 12:7).

I wonder if Paul's messenger from Satan quit tormenting him after
his third prayer. As I read the passage in 2 Corinthians 12, it seems to

me that Paul experienced a renewal of his mind and a settling of his heart about the thorn; perhaps he stopped praying for its removal and started valuing its God-redeemed purpose. He recounts the reply he received from God about the thorn's removal: "He said to me, 'My grace is sufficient for you, for my power is made perfect in weakness'" (v. 9). Leave it to God to turn things upside down from how we think they ought to be. To us, it makes sense to help people *out of* their misery, not *into* it. When our children come imploring us to pull the thorn out, we do not hesitate; but God often leaves it for purposes that he deems necessary.

As I have considered God's ways in my own sexual story and in those of other men, I am occasionally able to see things from a different perspective. Strategically drilled holes and carefully apportioned dynamite can create an explosion that leaves rubble and, to inexperienced eyes, little hope. To the casual observer our lives may look like devastation— broken marriages, sexually transmitted diseases, vengeful affairs, unquenchable selfishness, impenetrable darkness, despair. Yet every demolition expert understands that sometimes destruction is the path to progress.

THE LANGUAGE OF UNDESERVED ACCEPTANCE

It has taken many years, but I am beginning to believe the Scriptures that tell me God is not mad at me anymore. He is not waiting around for my next failure. Because of Jesus, I am not God's enemy—even when I fail. Ephesians 2:13-14 says it all: "But now in Christ Jesus you who once were far away have been brought near through the blood of Christ. For he himself is our peace . . . and has destroyed the barrier, the dividing wall of hostility."

I smile as I hear the echoes of a friend who was almost dancing as he proclaimed to me: "He really likes me! The God of all creation, my Father, really, really likes me!" I am still getting the hang of this truth about God's attitude toward me, but there are few things that bring more joy to my heart than this truth. I can't think of anything more crucial to transformation than understanding how completely the gospel changes us in the sight of God. Very little can change in a man's heart apart from hope, and hope is generated when a man stands in the presence of his Father, who is for him and not against him.

BEFORE HIS FACE

As I look back at how I wrestled with my sexuality and masculinity during my younger years, I am very hopeful and thankful because God has transformed me in unmistakable ways. Unfortunately I can't explain the process he used to transform me. What I do know is that he didn't necessarily answer my urgent, pain-filled questions. Rather he gave me his presence and stretched my small imagination and opened my heart to see him and to love him more fully. I am fortunate because I had trustworthy friends who listened to my story, heard my heart and didn't run away. I have the boundless gift of Sandy, my wife, as my best friend, confidante and lover; her belief in the strength of my heart along with her own desire to grow have been the healing kindnesses of God during our years together. And I have beautiful children who teach me daily about God's love and the limitations of my understanding as his child. I spent years wanting answers, and it was not until I laid down the questions in surrender and faith that I was able to begin seeing what he was really after.

C. S. Lewis closes *Till We Have Faces* with these words, which reflect well where I have found solace in my journey, and I offer them to you as a pointer to a larger truth I have come to see as central to abiding change. "I know now, Lord, why you utter no answer. You are yourself the answer. Before your face questions die away. What other answer would suffice?"[3] Lewis obviously understood God's word to Paul: "My grace is sufficient for you, for my power is made perfect in weakness" (2 Corinthians 12:9). We are transformed when we encounter and abide before the face of our Father.

PRACTICALLY SPEAKING

I have been changed inside and out. How? My experience is that through Christ God gives us the opportunity to become more fully ourselves—better warriors, lovers and friends: unique reflections of his likeness. I challenge you to take a closer look at your own sexual story that you too might be changed inside out. It is a journey worth taking.

Here are some practical ways of receiving the transforming work only God can do.

Refuse to lose hope. Perhaps your efforts are exhausted, but God's aren't. Know that in your weakest moments, his Spirit is praying for you (see Romans 8:26). Usually, the best resources aren't accessible to us until we come to the very end of our own. The Bible is replete with stories of circumstances that seemed hopeless until God entered the picture.

Pursue the full truth. Be as honest as you can with yourself, God and at least one other person, and when you've been as honest as you know how, go deeper still. Truth goes deep, but many of us only scratch the surface. In my experience of leading men to think through their own sexual stories I have found that the more honest a man becomes about his struggles, the greater the likelihood that he'll find health and healing. Secrets hollow out and suffocate the hearts of men; truth, even the most devastating truth, is fodder for a transforming fire.

Be in community. Mentors, counselors, trusted family members and wise and growing friends are vital to the process of transformation. We need others in order to grow up and out of our current places of immaturity. Most of the time we need others to point to the greater good that could be ours. Good communities can encourage our faith in Christ when it wanes; they can help us persevere when we are tempted to do otherwise. Good friends in faith comfort, challenge and rekindle our hearts.

Pursue the path of strong and intimate love. The sexual act was designed for relationship, not isolation. Sexual union grafts two people together and is designed by God to bond the bodies, souls, minds and strengths of two individuals for the purposes of reflecting his own love in union. Providing intimacy, mutuality and support to the other person are the goals of sexuality, not just our pleasure. Learn that no matter where you are on the path of coming to grips with your sexuality, you can always find a way to offer the grace of Christ to those around you. And this is done most intimately through possessing yourself for the sake of Christ as an instrument of love and encouragement.

Worship God more than your goals. I have found that getting questions answered and bringing an end to sexual struggles is often a very compelling goal, one bearing immense relational and generational consequences if it is not achieved. We want the affair to end with little consequence. We want to have more sexual fire in us. We want someone to just love us the way we want. We yearn for our spouses to forgive our improprieties and trust us completely again. We want our wives to cooperate with our sexual imagination and give us a little heaven on earth. We want what we are aroused by to be more wholesome and less frequent in our thoughts. But relief from struggle is not a worthy enough goal for any man, and this is perhaps why the relief often eludes us.

Ultimately, the pleasure found in our sexual pursuits, no matter how honorable and good, will always pale in comparison to the pleasure of finding and making peace with God, the greatest transformational pursuit of all. Our sex lives can be enemies or allies in our journey toward understanding and being changed by the kindness of the Father. Be well loved by him, love well and you will find your deepest desires.

9

MARRIAGE

LOVING THE HEART OF A WOMAN

Gary D. Chapman

Someone once told me marriage is like flies on a window pane. The flies on the inside are trying to get out and those on the outside are trying to get in.

I can identify with that picture. For months leading up to my wedding I could hardly wait to be married. I was in graduate school at the time, and I dreamed about how wonderful it was going to be. I had visions of coming home in the evening and studying in our own apartment. I could picture her sitting on the couch; when I would finish studying, I would look up and our eyes would meet. *Won't that be wonderful?* I thought. *A wife right there in the apartment!*

After we got married I found out that my wife didn't want to sit on the couch and watch me study. While I worked she would go downstairs and socialize with people in the apartment complex. I would sit there thinking, *This is just like it was before we got married. The only difference—that dorm room was a whole lot cheaper than this place.*

Before we got married I had this vision that at about 10:30 every night we would go to bed together. Wow! Going to go to bed every night with a woman! Wow! But after we got married, I found out that it had never crossed her mind to go to bed at 10:30. Right about that time of night she was just getting back from visiting the neighbors, and then she'd read a book until midnight. I'm thinking, *Why didn't you read while I was reading? Then we could go to bed together!*

Before we got married, I had this idea that everybody gets up when the sun gets up. But after we got married, I found out that my wife doesn't do mornings.

It didn't take me long not to like my wife, and it didn't take her long not to like me. And we succeeded in being utterly miserable.

God did not create marriage to make us miserable; he knew that together we would accomplish more for his kingdom than we would as individuals. He created us for each other. However, the purpose of life is not to have a good marriage. The meaning of life is to know God and to fulfill the purposes he created us for. In his plan for most people, marriage plays a major role in accomplishing that purpose. Even the hard times are used by God for good.

Most of the men I have talked with over the past thirty years had high expectations when they got married. Life was going to be beautiful. But slowly (or quickly, in some cases) they experienced disappointment. Most of the men who I've seen in my office were there because they were extremely unhappy with the quality of their marriage, and they blamed their wives for their unhappiness. They hoped that I could do something to change her behavior. They had hidden thoughts that they had married the wrong person.

I have had great empathy with these men because I know what it is to be married and miserable. Unfortunately, my marriage didn't turn around overnight. I don't know if we had marriage counselors back then, but I never heard of one. I don't know if we had Christian books on marriage, but I never saw one. Everyone told me that if you are a Christian and in love, then in marriage you *will* be happy. Well, I was a Christian and I was in love—at least before I got married I was in love. But I was a long way from happiness. My Christian view of marriage wouldn't allow me to entertain the thought of divorce, though I fully understood why others would pursue that option.

Being a problem-solver by nature, I set out to convince my wife that we could have a good marriage if she would just listen to me. But she wasn't open to my ideas. We often argued over issues, but most of the time we lived in silent suffering. I know what it is to be married and have the recurring thought, *I married the wrong person. How could I have made such a huge mistake? Surely if she were God's choice for me, things would not be this miserable.* The thought never crossed my mind in those days that God might want to use my pain to turn my heart toward him.

THE ATTITUDE OF CHRIST

I remember the day that in desperation I cried out to God: "I've done everything I know to do and my marriage is not getting any better. In fact, if anything, it's getting worse. I don't know what else to do." I have never heard anything clearer than what came to my mind: "Why don't you read the life of Jesus?"

I responded, "Read the life of Jesus? I am in seminary. I have read the life of Jesus many times."

I heard it again: "Why don't you read the life of Jesus?"

So I said, "All right. It was written in Greek, right?" By this time, I had twenty-seven academic hours in the Greek language. "OK, I'll read the life of Jesus in Greek." And I added, "If I have missed anything, please show me."

I worked my way through Matthew, Mark, Luke and John in Greek. What I discovered I could have discovered in any English translation. I don't know how I missed it all those years. I discovered the greatest leader the world has ever known. Even many non-Christians agree that no one has influenced human history as positively as has Jesus of Nazareth.

I didn't find Jesus barking out orders and telling his followers what they needed to do to make him happy. I found him rather on his knees, washing the feet of his followers. When he finished, he stood up and said, "I am your leader. And in my kingdom, this is the way you lead. In the Gentile world, the leader lords it over the others. But in my kingdom, the leader will serve the others. The greatest leader will be the greatest servant" (see John 13:1-17).

I had gone about my marriage in exactly the opposite manner. I had expected my wife to serve me. I had told her what she needed to do to be a good wife and expected her to comply—since I was the God-ordained leader in our marriage. In desperation I cried out to God, "Give me the attitude of Christ toward my wife. Teach me how to serve her in the same manner that Christ served his followers." In retrospect, it was the most significant prayer I've ever prayed. That prayer was the turning point in our marriage.

When I was willing to ask three simple questions, our marriage began to improve: (1) What could I do to help you? (2) How could I make your life easier? (3) How could I be a better husband to you? Do you know what I found out? When I was willing to ask those questions, my wife was willing to give me an answer. She had no interest in my washing her feet, but she had a lot of other good ideas.

When I let my wife teach me how I could serve her, do you know what happened? Not overnight but in time, she began to reciprocate. And when she did, I found myself with positive feelings toward her again. I distinctly remember the night I looked at her and thought, *I wouldn't mind touching her again if I thought she would let me."* I wasn't about to ask but I had the thought, *I wouldn't mind if she wouldn't mind.*

Today, and for many years now, I have an incredible wife. We have been walking the road of sacrificial service for a long time now—I have reached out to serve her and she has reached out to serve me. I said to her the other day, "If every woman in the world were like you, there would never be divorce." Why would a man leave a woman who is doing everything she can to encourage him and help him accomplish what he believes God has called him to do? And my goal through all these years has been to serve my wife so well that when I'm gone, she won't find another man who'll treat her the way I've treated her. The woman is going to miss me! There is no way to improve God's design: husband and wife giving their lives away to each other.

Karolyn and I were eating dinner the other night and began reflecting on the early days of our marriage. She said, "I used to feel guilty for the way I treated you in those early years, but I don't feel guilty anymore. I know God has forgiven me and I know God used all of that to make you the man you've become. You wouldn't have written the books or helped the people you've helped had it not been for the struggle of those early years." I smiled and said, "You are right. Thank you for making my life miserable!"

In modern Western society, perhaps nowhere has marital confusion reigned more than in the area of the husband's role. On one extreme is the dominant husband, who feels it's his responsibility to inform his wife as to what they are going to do and doesn't tolerate questions from his wife. On the other extreme is the distant husband, who expects the wife to support the family and make all the major decisions while he is the resident sports information source and, of course, while he keeps his muscles bulging with workouts at the local gym so his wife will be "proud of him."

Somewhere between these two is a healthy middle road where the husband is responsible, dependable and deeply committed to his wife and family—a loving leader. On the one hand, he is in touch with his feelings and is able to express pain and joy, sympathy and encouragement. He is able to relate to his wife on an emotional level. On the other hand, he is strong and intent on the well-being of his wife and family. He doesn't run when things get tough but looks for solutions that will benefit the whole family. He values the partnership of his wife. He wants to be there for her, but he has no desire to dominate her. This is the husband described in the Bible.

Let me share with you six characteristics of a loving husband. These are the insights God worked in my heart to turn my marriage in his direction.

1. A loving husband views his wife as a partner. A wife is not a trophy to be won in courtship and then placed on the wall for all to observe along with our ten-point buck. She's a living person with whom to have a relationship. She is not to be dominated and controlled to satisfy our own goals. She is to be known; God has plans for her. She is not a child to be patronized; she is a partner with whom her husband is developing a relationship.

God's word for Eve was *helper* or *partner.* In marriage the man and the woman become partners. Our differences mean that we each bring something unique to the table, but we come to the table as equals. The husband who doesn't view his wife as an equal partner will never be a loving leader. Partnership is to permeate the entire marriage. The husband will take initiative in creating an atmosphere where this partnership can be played out without undue tension. He assures his wife that he sees her as a partner and deeply desires her input on decisions.

2. A loving husband communicates with his wife. Life is shared primarily by means of communication, particularly discussing our thoughts, feelings and desires. One of a wife's deepest desires is to know her husband. When a husband goes long periods without talking about what he thinks and feels, she has the sense that he is shutting her out, and she feels isolated. She may guess what is going on in her husband's mind by his behavior, but unless that behavior is a pattern that he has exhibited with certain thoughts and desires previously, she is not likely to guess correctly. The old saying, "I can read him like a book" is simply not true.

Sometimes a wife stifles her husband's communication with an argumentative spirit or judgmental responses. Some time ago a husband said to me, "I've just stopped sharing my thoughts with my wife because every time I do, she pounces on it. She either disagrees with it or questions me about it and gives me a different perspective. It's as though I am not allowed to have a thought that she doesn't want to scrutinize. I would like to tell her my thoughts if she would simply accept them as my thoughts."

After two counseling sessions, it became obvious that part of the problem was his own defensiveness. Having had his ideas put down as a child, he had consciously determined that as an adult, his ideas would always be right; thus he became defensive whenever his wife or anyone else questioned his ideas. Part of the problem also lay in his wife's obsession with evaluating ideas and discussing each one to the final conclusion, proving one to be right and the other to be wrong. This pattern of communication is very stifling. Whatever stops the flow of your communication needs to be discovered and eliminated. If you can do this by discussion between the two of you, fine. If not, then it is advisable to discuss it with a friend or to go for professional counseling. Both hyperdefensiveness and extreme scrutiny typically need the help of a counselor to bring the couple to understand what is going on and to change the patterns. The loving husband will take the initiative in getting such counseling if needed.

We can't afford to let communication come to a halt or to allow communication to be simply the battlefield on which we fight out our differences. Communication involves listening fully as much as talking. The loving husband will take initiative to understand his wife's thoughts, desires and feelings. He will listen empathetically, not judgmentally. Even when he disagrees with her, he will allow her to express herself and seek to understand her perspective. Positive, open, free, accepting communication is the characteristic of a healthy marriage. The loving leader must take the initiative in seeing that this kind of communication becomes a way of life.

3. A loving husband puts his wife at the top of his priority list. All of us live by priorities. They are revealed most fully by our actions. Answer the questions, How do I spend my time? How do I invest my money? How do I use my energy? and your list of priorities will emerge.

In Western society, vocation ranks near the top of the list for most men. This is not necessarily in conflict with a man's relationship with his wife unless the vocation comes to possess him. One wife complained, "He's married to his job. I only get the leftovers. If we have an evening planned together and his boss calls, our evening is over. The boss has the priority." When our vocation controls us and controls our plans for marriage enrichment, it has become our number one priority. And it can eventually destroy our marriage. People are more important than things. The loving husband will not allow his vocation to supplant time with his wife.

Husbands often feel that their children have replaced them in their wife's eyes. This is a legitimate concern, and in truth it is often the case. But it may also be true of the husband, particularly in a marriage where his emotional needs are not adequately met by his wife, or he feels somewhat estranged from her. He may find himself focusing more time and energy on his children because he is receiving more feedback from them. A loving husband will recognize this behavior as dysfunctional and take steps to refocus his time and energy on meeting the needs of his wife and helping her learn how, in turn, to meet his needs.

4. A loving husband seeks his wife's best interests regardless of her response. Modern thinking is more contractual: I will love you if you will love me. We tend to be egocentric, even in marriage. The focus of our effort is to get our own needs met. In fact, much of modern psychology has emphasized this as normal behavior. Some have gone so far as to say that *all* of our behavior toward others is motivated by getting our own needs met.

Unconditional love, on the other hand, focuses on meeting the needs of the other person. In marriage, this means the husband looks out for the wife's best interest, supporting her in her endeavors even when he may not totally agree with them. It means helping her reach her goals and aspirations because he values her as a person. It's not "I will wash the dishes if you will give me sex." It's "I will wash the dishes because I know you are tired."

Far too many husbands sit back and think, *When she decides to become affectionate; when she decides to think about my needs; when she decides to be more responsive to me, then I'll start loving her.* When a husband takes this attitude, he is neither loving nor leading. God loved us while we were yet sinners (Romans 5:8). As leaders in our marriage, we may be called on to do the same for our wives.

It is fairly easy to love a wife who is loving you, but to love an unloving wife may be the greatest challenge a husband ever faces. This is where spiritual transformation becomes essential. Loving the unlovely is a godlike characteristic, and the ability to do so must come from God. The good news is that he is fully ready and capable of giving us that ability. The apostle Paul said, "God has poured out his love into our hearts by the Holy Spirit" (Romans 5:5). When we make ourselves a willing channel, God will use us to express his love to our spouses. This is what I experienced after I prayed, "Lord, give me the attitude of Christ toward my wife." Unconditional love for your wife is the most powerful influence you can have on her. And God stands ready to make this a reality in your life.

5. A loving husband is committed to discovering and meeting his wife's needs. Perhaps this seems redundant in the light of what I have just said about unconditional love, but it has been my observation through the years that many husbands simply don't understand the needs of their wives. Consequently, in their ignorance they make no effort to meet those needs. Some husbands believe that if they work at a steady job and bring home a decent salary, they have completed their role as a husband. They have little concept of a wife's emotional and social needs.

Most wives appreciate their husband's hard work and his efforts to provide for the physical needs of the family. But this is only foundational and fundamental; it's not the final word. Her emotional need for love, affection, tenderness, kindness and encouragement are as fundamental to her emotional health as is food to her physical health.

The husband who is satisfied with simply putting food on the table has a very limited view of the importance of his role as husband. Once the food is on the table, it's time to nurture his wife's inner needs. Her most basic emotional need is the need to feel loved.

Many years ago I discovered that what makes a husband feel loved is not necessarily what makes a wife feel loved. After twenty years of marriage counseling, I concluded that there are five fundamental languages of love: five ways to express love emotionally. Each language has many dialects, but the fundamental languages of love are words of affirmation, acts of service, gift-giving, quality time, and physical touch.

Each of us has a primary love language. One of the five speaks more deeply to us than the other four. The husband who wishes to meet his wife's need for emotional love must discover his wife's primary love language and speak it regularly. Once he is speaking her primary love language, he can sprinkle in the other four. His wife will feel loved consistently, and chances are she'll greatly admire and respond to this husband who is meeting this need.

Her need for security is also fundamental. First, it's a physical need, but her greatest security is the need for the deep assurance that her husband is committed to her. The husband who threatens his wife with the words of divorce or off-handedly makes comments like: "You'd be better off with somebody else" or "I think I'll find someone else" is playing into the hands of the enemy. The loving husband will make every effort to communicate to his wife that whatever happens, he is with her. If there are disagreements, he will take the time to listen, understand and seek resolution. If she suffers physical or emotional pain, he will be by her side.

6. A loving husband models his spiritual and moral values. All men have a set of beliefs about what is right and wrong, and a set of beliefs about what exists beyond the material world. The husband's spiritual and moral beliefs must be modeled by his life. The greater the gap between what he proclaims to believe on these issues and what he actually does, the greater the disrespect he engenders. But if the wife sees his life as being consistent with what he says he believes, she will respect him even if she disagrees with his beliefs.

This doesn't mean that the husband must be perfect. It does mean that he must make a conscientious effort to apply his spiritual and moral beliefs to his own lifestyle. When he fails, he must be willing to acknowledge his failure and ask forgiveness. It is in this act of confession that he demonstrates that his beliefs are strong and genuine, and that he won't excuse himself for wrong behavior. Such authenticity will have a positive influence on his wife.

THE CHRISTLIKE HUSBAND

Not many women will run away from the man who is lovingly leading her. Some time ago I did a little research and discovered that not a single wife in U.S. history has murdered her husband while he was washing the dishes!

God's desire for all of us is spiritual maturity, which means Christlikeness. Nothing measures the Christian husband's true spirituality better than the way he treats his wife. This is why the content of this book is so important in the life of a man. When a wife sees the transformation of a man's heart, she is drawn to be intimate with that man. As you are seeking to grow in the other areas discussed in this book, a byproduct will be a more intimate marriage. God ordained you to be the *loving leader* in your marriage. Don't ever separate those two words. The Christlike leader is committed to serving the needs of his wife, not demanding that she meet his needs. Christ alone is the model of headship, and his method of leadership was service, even to the point of death. May God give all of us the attitude of Christ toward our wives.

10

PARENTING

BEING LIKE JESUS TO OUR CHILDREN

D. Ross Campbell

I started my fathering career when I was too young and immature to be a father—a rather common arrangement, don't you think? Now, as a father of four children and a grandfather to three, and having practiced child psychiatry for many years, I have to admit that most of what I know about parenting, I have learned the hard way.

I affirm your desire to fulfill what may well be your highest calling: being the best father possible. While our life circumstances may be different to one degree or another, I am confident that we share the same basic goals of giving our children a loving and secure childhood, and equipping them for the challenges of adulthood in a tumultuous and uncertain world.

MY EXPOSURE TO PARENTING

Like many of you, I came into fatherhood poorly equipped. While both of my parents were fine people whom I love and respect to this day, my childhood home could best be described as dysfunctional and chaotic. Emotional nurture was, for the most part, nonexistent. As a result, my siblings and I left home at the earliest opportunity, scattering in different directions across the country. (Fortunately, since we all have become much older, the strains of an unhappy childhood have eased enough for us to renew close relationships with one another.)

Emerging from adolescence with a longing for some sense of order and structure, I applied to the U.S. Naval Academy and successfully received an appointment. In my first year at Annapolis, I accepted Christ as my Lord and Savior. This was through the ministry of the Officers' Christian Fellowship, a wonderful organization in all of the military services and the service academies. In fact, the Naval Academy was so spiritually nourishing for me that I wanted to go into the ministry during my senior year. But the Navy (and the Lord) had other plans for me.

Pat and I were married right after my graduation from the Naval Academy. We were quite amazed when she became pregnant on our honeymoon. So there I was—a newly commissioned naval officer, newly married and a new father at the grand old age of twenty-two.

As a new father, I was excited, of course, but totally unprepared—anxious and scared—for this wonderful but awesome responsibly. To make matters worse, my ship was scheduled for a six-month deployment to the Far East four months after we were married. I was having a difficult time handling all of this. I had to send Pat home when the ship set sail, which nearly killed me. I didn't see my first child, Carey, until she was three months old.

Because of the constant Soviet threat, it was necessary for us to be at sea 85 percent of the time. And I felt the Lord wanted me to be the best naval officer I could be. I was on ships that fought the Chinese in China, put down civil war in Lebanon, and escorted the president on his visit to Japan. The most harrowing experience, though, was on the destroyer escort USS Daniel A. Joy (DE 585). I was gunnery officer on that ship at the time Khrushchev sent to Cuba three vessels loaded with intercontinental nuclear missiles. When we intercepted these Soviet ships, they tried to plow right through us. After warning them three times to turn around, we were one hundred yards astern of the lead ship. As gunnery officer, I was ordered by the captain to load all guns and aim them at the Soviet ship. I was the one who would have given the order that no doubt would have started World War III. As I stood there, I had the strange feeling that history was being made and I was a part of it. I also felt God's presence and his wonderful peace and assurance. Suddenly the Soviet ship turned around and departed. I deeply believe that God saved the world from destruction that day.

Living through this experience and many others, I grew in my faith. I was also fortunate to be in touch with mature Christian mentors, including missionaries in the countries my ships visited. My growing faith and my mentors saved my children from an overly strict, possibly harsh father. It has taken me many years of learning to come to the place where I feel I have a right to hand out any advice.

SPIRITUAL WARFARE

Our culture has radically changed, especially in the last ten years. It has become extremely difficult for a parent to raise children with good character, integrity and an appropriate set of morals, including such basic values as telling the truth, keeping promises (especially sacred promises such as marriage vows) and taking responsibility for their own behavior. These once-basic values have largely disappeared.

In the recent past our culture helped parents to train their children in basic values and the appropriate ways to manage anger. But today most of our society's influences on our children are negative and obviously anti-Christian. Think, for example, of the refreshing, often inspiring sitcoms that taught values, especially to children. Now think of the sitcoms today emphasizing sex, violence and the near-worship of those who manipulate and harm others.

At one time, when a child had problem, as a child psychiatrist I could generally tell what kind of home that child came from. Not today. A problem child or teenager can come from any type of home, including a dedicated Christian home. This is because of the cultural shift. Tragically, most parents are not fully aware of this radical cultural change. But even if they are, they don't know how to combat its unwholesome influences. Fellow father, we are in a war, a spiritual and cultural war! And at the present time we are losing dreadfully. A wise father must know how to appropriately raise children in this culture. Very few do.

Some fathers have overreacted to the liberalizing atmosphere of our culture. But the wise Christian father will be wary of extreme and unusual teachings on parenting. Sadly these have taken root among conservative Christian parents. Rather than discussing each of these unhealthy, destructive methods of parenting, we'll talk about what your child needs from you to become the person you and the Lord want him or her to become.

Fathers must understand five critical needs of every child:

1. loving discipline
2. unconditional love
3. protection from the harmful influences of our culture
4. anger management
5. knowing God

Today's parents increasingly are having problems with their children because of the unhealthy influences of our culture in each of these areas. A wise father understands this and carefully meets his child's needs in these five areas. If the child is deprived of needs in one of these areas, he or she will suffer greatly—and so will the father. Let's take an extended look at the five critical needs.

LOVING DISCIPLINE

As a new father, almost all of what I knew about discipline was based on the military model, which goes something like this: Conduct that meets or exceeds expectations and is outstanding and exemplary is acceptable. But the slightest error suffers serious consequences.

Military discipline is based on a school of thought known as behavior modification, which uses a system of rewards and punishments. Interestingly, there is a current trend among Christian authors and teachers to embrace behavior modification as the model for successful Christian parenting.[1] Undoubtedly, this is a well-intentioned reaction to a regrettable societal decline in moral values, civility and discipline. In these models, there's much discussion of the negative effects of "sparing the rod and spoiling the child" (see Proverbs 13:24), but our Lord's central teaching about unconditional love is ignored. Unfortunately, because behavior modification is geared toward controlling outward behavior without taking into account the emotional and psychological needs of the child, it can have disastrous consequences.

Of course, it's ridiculous to expect military-like behavior in a child. But I did, and most men, whether they realize this or not, do too. When we are young fathers, we usually see things in black and white. Our expectations are rigid and narrow. The mature man, on the other hand, is willing to modify his stance if his ideas are proven to be in error. Though solid in his basic values, self-identity and security in God, a mature man is flexible. My deepening understanding of Scripture saved my children from an overly strict and potentially harsh father. Scripture taught me that children are made in the image of God (Genesis 1:26), and they need to be handled with care: "Fathers, do not exasperate your children; instead, bring them up in the training and instruction of the Lord (Ephesians 6:4).

Look at how Jesus approached children. Matthew 19:13-14 says, "Then little children were brought to Jesus for him to place his hands on them and pray for them. But the disciples rebuked those who brought them. Jesus said, 'Let the little children come to me, and do not hinder them, for the kingdom of heaven belongs to such as these.' " Mark 10:16 goes on: "And he took the children in his arms, put his hands on them and blessed them." And we are taught in Psalm 127:3: "Children [are] a reward from him." This helped me to see my role of fathering in a more mature and loving way.

Fathers are not omnipotent. Our power is quite limited. If we consistently use our power in a negative and dictatorial manner, our authority will become less and less effective with our children, and eventually we will have none left. A father should always make the most positive, loving, teaching choice he can. This will foster a loving, comfortable relationship with his child. Our children know when we have a choice in how we discipline and teach them. When they see us taking the high ground, using loving and positive ways to train them, they will return our love.

Many parents are aware of only one way to manage a child's behavior—punishment. In truth, there are five ways to help a child mature: requests, commands, gentle physical manipulation, punishment and behavior modification. A wise father will learn how and when to use each of them in ways to help his children.

Requests are the most positive response because they calm a child. *Commands* are of course sometimes necessary, but they tend to arouse anger and anxiety in most children. *Gentle physical manipulation* means taking your child in your hands and gently guiding him or her. It's positive discipline because it conveys a sense of sincere caring and gentleness to the child.

Punishment is the most negative child-rearing technique. Of course, a father must be ready to use it when appropriate, but it's difficult to use correctly. Punishment must always fit the misbehavior, and the particular punishment used with one child may not work with another. And using inappropriate punishment for a child will do more harm than good.

Another danger with using punishment is related to the parent's mood. If a parent is having a wonderful day and punishment is required, the punishment will most likely be too lenient, and the child may not learn his or her lesson. On the other hand, if a parent is having a dreadful day, the punishment will most likely be too harsh, and the child will grow resentful. If the punishment is extremely harsh, the child will may never forget it.

Even though using *behavior modification* too much in parenting, especially as the primary way to train a child, is disastrous, it can be used for specific behavioral problems with good effect. For more information of the positive uses of behavior modification I recommend the book *Don't Be Afraid to Discipline* by Ruth Peters.

UNCONDITIONAL LOVE

Children (and everyone else for that matter) learn best by observing good role models. Our goal as parents should be to model the behavior we expect of our children. Of course, this is more difficult than simply telling a child what to do and using rewards and punishment as incentives. But modeling is much more successful.

Scripture's influence on my parenting. I began fathering with military-like discipline, but as I studied Scripture, I learned how Jesus wanted me to love as a father. Counterbalancing the rigid discipline that had become so much a part of my life, Scripture taught me that God presented himself to us as our loving Father. And Jesus modeled his relationship to the Father for us. God offers us unmerited grace, limitless forgiveness and an overriding and overwhelming gift of unconditional love.

As a Christian I was loved despite my sins, shortcomings and failures. Thus I determined that, above all else, I would try to convey to my children a similar sense of love. I loved them not because of their beauty, athleticism, intelligence or talent, but because they too are God's children. I loved them in spite of their failures or deficiencies. This is how God the Father loves me, and this is how Scripture teaches me to love my own children.

As my daughter grew, I realized that she needed to be taught how to love. And this depended on her need to *feel* loved. From Scripture, I understood that it was *my* responsibility to teach her these lessons. And the only true way that lasts a lifetime is to teach her by example.

There are three basic ways keep your child's emotional tank full with unconditional love: eye contact, physical contact, and focused attention.

- Loving eye contact is looking pleasantly into the eyes of your child as the child is looking into yours. As simple as this seems, it's a powerful way to transfer your heartfelt love to your child. Research shows that most parents fail to do this simple act of love. In fact, when most parents do make eye contact with their children, it's to convey negative feelings. Give your child plenty of loving eye contact.

- Physical contact, you would think, is a natural way to love a child. But again research shows that most parents don't express their love physically. Physical contact is more than hugs and kisses. Of course hugging and kissing are nice and should be done when appropriate. But just as important are such things as a gentle touch on the back of the shoulder or arm, or jostling the child's hair.

- Giving a child focused attention means spending enough time with the child that he or she feels like the most important person in the world to you. While eye contact and physical contact take almost no effort on the part of the parent, focused attention takes extra effort. It involves the sacrifice of your time. But it's worth it.

Finding adequate time to focus on my child is one of the greatest problems in my fathering experience. The only way that I have been able to carve out this time for my kids is to schedule it in my appointment book several weeks in advance. Then, when another obligation or request arises, I simply say, "I'm sorry but I have another appointment scheduled at that time."

A pearl of wisdom. Our children know when there is more than one way to discipline them. And they know whether we choose the more loving and more positive, and are unbelievably thankful. This is one way to actually generate love in the heart of your child. Let's look at a couple of examples.

Say your boy is playing in the yard, hits a ball and breaks a window. You can respond in several ways: ignore it, angrily chew-out your son, physically punish him, deprive him of something, or help him to repair the window. Of course the more positive and loving option is obvious. Your son will remember working with you for the rest of his life.

Learning from Dale. I had been gone from home for three days when Dale, my youngest son, was five years old. Pat and Dale were at the airport to meet me when I returned. I was so anxious to talk with Pat that I inadvertently ignored Dale. He repeatedly tried to get my attention, but I said something like "I need to talk to your mother—just hold your horses" in a less than kind voice. By the time we got home, my usually sweet, people-pleasing child had the whole family in turmoil. His behavior had deteriorated to the point where I was on the verge of spanking him.

Then Pat whispered to me, "Why don't you practice what you preach?" I was on the verge of punishing my boy when I was misbehaving myself. An empty emotional tank is indeed the most common cause of misbehavior in a young child. I wasn't fulfilling my basic responsibilities as a Christian father. I forgot that I can prevent serious mistakes such as this by asking myself, *What does my child need?* Then I can correct the problem behavior positively rather than by using punishment.

Dale needed his daddy. Through his misbehavior, Dale was asking me, "Do you love me? You won't even talk to me. Don't you love me anymore?" I took Dale to our bedroom and held him. I filled his emotional tank with eye contact, physical contact and focused attention. After $3\frac{1}{2}$ minutes, he was his usual, lovable, sweet self.

PROTECTION FROM THIS TROUBLED CULTURE

Our culture has changed so radically that if a person from even the recent past visited, he or she would be totally shocked. One of the worst aspects is that most fathers are unsure of their ability to parent, and this insecurity deeply affects their child's self-esteem and sense of security. The home atmosphere is where a child thrives, or not. Any father can be a good, effective parent. And this is critical because the father must feel good about his parenting. Only then can the home atmosphere be one where the child can grow to be his or her best.

Finding adequate time to focus on my child is one of the greatest problems in my fathering experience.

Most fathers today are insecure about their parenting because of fear—fear of the world their children are entering. Therefore fathers can't relax; they're tense and uptight with their children. This in turn causes children to be insecure and anxious—two of greatest curses we can inflict on them.

We can know that we are competent fathers by parenting biblically, logically and rationally. Then we will know that what we are thinking and doing is right. Best of all, when we know that we are a good fathers, we can relax—we can enjoy our children, and they can enjoy us and truly develop to be their very best.

Children need to feel secure. The marriage relationship is critical to a child's welfare. It can make the difference between a happy, productive life and one filled with problems and pain. Fathers must love their child's mother, not only for the mother's sake but also for the child's. But our culture no longer supports strong marriages, and I have seen the disastrous results when a father fails to love his child's mother well.

The greatest test of manhood is how well a man loves his life partner. Mark was a surgery resident at the same time I did my psychiatric residency. Mark and his wife, Jane, had three girls.

When our residency days were over, we moved to different cities. After about five years we received the distressing news that Mark was divorcing Jane. As though that wasn't bad enough, we were informed that Mark had abused Jane, and the kids were having severe problems. Mark and Jane had a wholesome, wonderful family until Mark failed in his responsibilities and commitments to his children's mother.

All men are faced with sexual temptation. But often the temptation is the greatest when a man is in his forties. A wise father must be prepared for this almost inevitable temptation. We need our Christian brothers to pray for us and to hold us accountable. If we blindly assume yielding to temptation could never happen to us, we are fools. A disaster such as this must be avoided at all costs. Honor God, your children's mother and yourself by preparing yourself to resist temptation. You will save your children some of the worst problems in life. But if you do fall, go to the Lord, confess your sin and be forgiven and cleansed (see 1 John 1:9) so that you can restore your relationship to those you are responsible for.

You are undoubtedly aware of other unhealthy influences in our society: music, movies, television, video games, school policies and so on. There are extremely few areas left that provide wholesome outlets and entertainment for our children. Unhealthy material streams into our homes through a variety of media. Fathers need to be extremely vigilant on behalf of their children. Equip the television and Internet with child-protection devices; keep the computer and the TV where it's difficult for a child to use alone. Be proactive in how you protect your children and prepare them to face the temptations that will inevitably present themselves.

In Matthew 10:16 Jesus said to his disciples, "I send you out as sheep in the midst of wolves: Therefore be wise as serpents and harmless as doves" (NKJV). A wise father will take this verse to heart. Our children are harmless as doves all right, but they are not wise as serpents. It is our responsibility to pass wisdom on to them.

TRAIN YOUR CHILD TO HANDLE ANGER MATURELY

Anger has become one of the greatest problems in our changing society. Our culture used to help parents train their children to handle anger properly. Not today. Our present culture teaches children how to handle anger in the worst possible ways. Unless a child is trained to appropriately manage anger, he or she could develop anti-authority attitudes and possibly *reject the Christian faith itself*. Unfortunately, many parents don't realize that anger has become a major problem in and outside of our homes.

Even if parents are aware of this problem, most don't know how to deal with it. Wise fathers must understand this problem and its ramifications for their children, learning how to train their children to handle anger maturely. This is one of the greatest gifts fathers can give their children.

It's important to begin early in training children to manage their anger. A child's character gradually develops during childhood and adolescence. But around the age of sixteen, his or her character begins to harden and thereafter becomes extremely difficult to change. Whether or not a child is trained to handle anger during his or her early years usually determines how well the child's character is formed.

All children naturally express their anger verbally, which is *unpleasant*. In response, most parents become upset and respond to their child in anger. Among the many ways to encourage children to develop negative attitudes toward authority, dumping anger on them is the worst.

When a child verbally expresses anger and is not acting out, we should rejoice! He or she is ready to be trained. Permit your child to express anger verbally, and listen patiently. Remember that the child only has two options for expressing anger: verbally or behaviorally. Of course, verbal anger, while unpleasant, is always preferred.

We shouldn't permit a child to verbalize anger *all* the time. There are two instances when a child shouldn't be allowed to express anger verbally: when the child (1) is being aggressive or (2) is ventilating. *Aggression* occurs when a child is attempting to do harm with anger. *Ventilation* is when a child is "letting it all hang out," yelling, screaming, pouting and so on for no legitimate reason. Children often do this to frustrate their parents so much that the parents give in and say something like, "All right, just go ahead and do it!"

When a child has fully expressed his or her anger verbally so it is out of his or her system, then the training begins. There are three steps to take. First, let your child know that you are pleased that he or she expressed anger verbally and not behaviorally. I used to say something like, "I'm so proud of you for bringing your anger to me verbally, Honey. I want to know when you are happy or unhappy, or even when you are angry."

Next, compliment your child for the things he or she has done right. Say something like this: "I'm so proud of the way you handled your anger. You didn't slam the door or take it out on your little brother or the dog. You simply told me that you were angry, and why. That's great!"

Third, help your child take the next step up the anger ladder. Say something like, "I'm proud of the way you are learning to manage your anger, Honey. And I have just one request. From now on, would you please not yell so loud when you express your anger to me?" Of course, the specific request you make depends on where your child needs to make the most improvement in the expression of anger.

There is much more to training a child in anger management, but using these three steps will help your child learn mature ways of handling anger. As a result, your son or daughter will have a healthy, positive approach to life.

I am so thankful that I didn't listen to those Christian "experts" who advocate punishment as the primary way to train a child. I cherish the times when my children chose to honestly share their opinions, thoughts, feelings, *and anger* with me rather than hide them because they feared punishment (see Proverbs 15:1; 29:11; Ephesians 6:4; James 1:19).

KNOWING GOD

In order to give our precious children a lifelong anchor in this world and the next, we fathers must possess a solid foundation on which to base our lives. Of course this foundation is what every heart craves: God himself—a personal relationship with God through his Son Jesus Christ. If we have this precious gift of grace, we can share it with our children *as we live it.* We must let our children observe our own spiritual growth, letting them share in our spiritual struggles and victories, all of course on a level that is appropriate for their age and understanding. Then we can invite them to share their own spiritual growth—both positive and negative—with us.

However, a mistake I made as a new Christian father was emphasizing their spiritual growth without first fulfilling their emotional needs. Many Christian fathers make the same mistake. Here is some advice: a great time to fulfill emotional needs *and* encourage spiritual growth is at bedtime. Most children desperately want their parents' attention at bedtime. It's a wonderful time to express love and bond emotionally. It's also a great time for stories, which are great teaching tools. Sharing your own spiritual walk and experiences, and reading about biblical characters and events, and applying them to your children's lives are profound ways to help them get a solid spiritual foundation. They'll learn to love and trust God (and you). Nothing is more wonderful than to see your children developing Christlike character and values.

Fathers, you can help your children grow to maturity by providing the necessary love and emotional support while introducing them to your loving Father and his Son Jesus.

MY GRATITUDE TO THE LORD

As I counsel parents who are having problems with their adult children, I sadly hear the same theme over and over. These fine people tell heartbreaking tales of how they followed the teachings of "experts" who advocated destructive ways to relate to a child. They all express how they wish they had spent more time loving their child. They wish they had been less harsh and more positive in their discipline, and had spent more time with their child. Not one parent has wished he or she had been more rigid in discipline.

Christian parents should be better exposed to sound teaching in biblical wisdom and scientifically researched principles. This is something you, as a Christian father, can help bring about. Won't you work toward this goal with me?

This is the first time I have written against the parenting advice of other Christian authors. It makes me uncomfortable, and I know that this is unappealing to most Christians. But the situation is almost desperate.

The number of children from Christian homes with severe problems has reached epidemic proportions, and Christian parents are increasingly using strange, extreme methods. Ironically, the very disciplinary methods that have helped create this negative situation are now being used to the extreme in an attempt to correct it. It's a vicious circle.

I need to add that I am a father who can truly say, "There but for the grace of God go I." God has mercifully transformed me, an ignorant, overly strict, incompetent father. Because of his grace, my children are emotionally and spiritually healthy, and they love Christ as their Lord and Savior. Are they perfect? No, but each is maturing in his or her walk of faith. This is what I hope for and pray that all Christian fathers experience.

THE CONFIDENT FATHER

A confident father is a wonderful thing to behold. And a confident father is a good father. Follow the principles in this chapter and other good parenting material, and your home will become one where your children can grow to be their best. Your home will be relaxed, laid back, filled with laughter and free of tension, fear and anxiety.

I pray that your fathering will be a great joy for you. I pray that your child will be everything God has planned for him or her to be. May his blessing be on you in this wondrous endeavor of fathering.

PART THREE

FORWARD

11

LEGACY

INVESTING IN THE FUTURE

Craig M. Glass

Get rid of your junk, or move!" Those unsettling words were spoken years ago when a village outside of Chicago took action against one of its citizens.

For generations a family had been living in a rural area on the outskirts of the city. It had now become engulfed by relentlessly expanding suburbs. The family had a business at their home—collecting, storing and selling junk.

This was more than just an odd lawnmower by the side of the house or a used car parked in the driveway. It was piles of rusting junk: tractors, washing machines, a forties-era Greyhound bus and the fuselage of a DC3 airplane.

Let's face it, if someone has a DC3 in their backyard, sooner or later it's going to start annoying the neighbors. This one certainly did.

Eventually the city gave the family a choice: either get rid of all their junk or move. The local newspaper interviewed the head of the household, asking him what he thought of the village's ultimatum. This was his response: "It's unfair! Our family has been collecting junk for years. It's all we know."

A lot of our families are like that. We collect wounded relational habits, dysfunctional communication patterns or sinful lifestyles. They become an accepted way of living that may, in fact, seem normal to us.

Not only do we collect them, we pass them on. Intentionally or not, they become our legacy to others.

Proverbs 13:22 touches on this concept. In *The Message* it says, "A good life gets passed on to the grandchildren." A godly man leaves a legacy for the next generations, for those who live beyond him, not just his children but those whose lives he touches every day—friends, neighbors, coworkers and family. They are the ones to whom a legacy is passed. A godly man leaves a good one. An unintentional man passes on junk.

Several years ago I had a transforming realization. I worked for an organization that trained and sent missionaries throughout the world. One of my responsibilities was determining who of those people were prepared for the demands of crosscultural ministry and who were not.

Working with these candidates, I started to see a recurring pattern. For those who were clearly hindered by relational or emotional issues the root of the matter almost always went back to their relationship with their father. They had "father wounds" that were not healed. This affected their view of themselves and their view of God, and they were still living with visible scars.

The lesson is inescapable. Men influence lives; we affect others for better or worse. That's why it is so important that we consider both the inheritance we received as well as the legacy we want to pass on.

Our inheritance is poured into us; our legacy pours out from us. God works in us and calls on us to transform our inheritance so that our legacy is a blessing, not simply the continuation of a curse.

We are all creating our own legacies. The key question is: What kind of legacy will it be?

WE RECEIVE AN INHERITANCE

Our inheritance is more than just a financial endowment. It's all of the factors that made us who we are today. It's what we receive from our "soil," most significantly our parents, our culture, our schools and our places of worship.

Part of our inheritance is the assumption that our way of doing life is mostly correct, and others' ways are varying degrees of wrong. Our parents may reinforce this through comments such as, "I don't care how others do it; *our* family does it this way." Certainly our churches place a strong emphasis on the rightness of their faith and practice. Other faiths or denominations are a little bit—or a lot—off.

This self-centered approach toward life and the convictions on which it is founded can become a part of the junk we collect and then pass on. Unless we open ourselves to the healing nature of transformation we'll pass on those same wounded convictions to others.

We had no say in determining our inheritance, but our legacy is ours to choose. Our legacy moves outward from us. It is the impact and influence that we pass on to others. Legacy is that part of us that lives in the lives of other people and continues to live once we're gone.

A few years ago I shared a truly powerful experience with my father. He grew up in a Christian family in an Irish neighborhood on Chicago's south side. One day he called and said, "I'm going down to my old neighborhood today and visiting my parent's gravesite. Do you want to come along?" Though I was in my forties, I had never seen his childhood home or the gravesite of my grandparents. I jumped at the opportunity and said, "I'd love to!"

Driving down the expressway to the South Side, I expected some new insights into that neighborhood. What I didn't anticipate was that we would be visiting my father's inheritance.

Finding the street where he grew up, we parked and looked at the houses lining the street. Dad pointed out his house and where he and his pals played softball and football in the street. He told me the names of all the families that lived there: the Sullivans, the Kellys, the Burkes, the McCredies. They were Irish immigrant families whose fathers worked as firemen, policemen or street workers.

By this time I was starting to get a different mental picture of my dad. I didn't see a man with white hair and wrinkles whose stride has shortened with arthritis, but a young, active boy with red hair and freckles, full of energy, playing sixteen-inch softball.

We drove over to his high school, Calumet High. Classes were not in session that day and the doors were open, so we walked down the halls and into the cafeteria. He said, "Over there in that corner, that's where I always ate lunch." I saw a red-haired boy eating a peanut butter sandwich, six decades ago.

As we went to the P.E. wing, we walked through a hallway with a collection of old photographs, one of which was the football team from 1940. There he was, the center, holding the football, my dad; he knew every name of those pictured—characters from a story told long ago.

I realized I had embarked on a trip into the past with my father; that he has a long and deep story; a story that is the preface of my own.

The most powerful part of that day was when we went to the cemetery where his dad and mom are buried. We found our way to the two gravesites and stood in silence, beneath the leafy canopy of a majestic oak tree, pondering those two lives that had made such a profound impact on my father's own: Neal Morgan Glass and Kathryn McLean Glass.

Finally, Dad asked, "Do you mind if I pray?" He prayed a relatively short prayer, but he ended with four words that have stood out to me ever since. He thanked the Lord for his family and for his father, and then he said, "I have no regrets." A man, almost eighty years old, who can say that he has no regrets. Remarkable.

I thought, *What a father my grandfather must have been.* I was moved to be closer to him somehow, so I knelt down next to Grandpa's gravestone. I just wanted to be in some kind of contact with this man who was a part of my story so long ago. He died when I was two or three years old; I only remember faint images of sitting on his bed just prior to his death. He called me, "My wee little man."

I placed my hands on his headstone and traced the letters of his name with my fingers. Neal Morgan Glass. I thought to myself, *Grandpa, thank you so much for being the kind of dad you were.* He was born in a dirt-floor cottage in Northern Ireland, moved to Chicago as a young man and spent his whole life as a streetcar motorman, driving the significant and the insignificant alike through the busy streets of the city.

He was not a wealthy man, not an important man in the world's eyes. Few would call his a "success story." Yet he provided for and raised a family; he was faithful to his wife and children; he was a godly man and he passed on a rich spiritual legacy to my father.

Standing there with Dad, I realized that perhaps he might want to be alone, so I went to the car and watched my father. I can still picture him standing silently over his parents' gravestones underneath that huge oak tree on a perfect summer day. The sun shining through the branches, etching shadows on the lawn, a cool breeze rustling the leaves.

When he returned to the car, I said, "Dad, I just want to let you know something . . ." I hardly even knew how to say what was on my heart. "I realized just now that someday that will be me standing under that oak tree, and I'll be looking at your headstone. Dad, I don't know if you're going to be able to see me, and I doubt you'll know what I'm thinking, but I want to tell you right now what will be on my mind. I'll be thanking God for you. I'll be thanking God for the kind of man and the kind of father you were. And I'll have four words on my mind. *I have no regrets.*"

Have I led a perfect life? Absolutely not. I've had disappointments and I've stumbled in a number of ways. Do I have perfect parents? No—great parents, but certainly not perfect. But I have a father who is faithful, who is present, who is loving, who received an unusual inheritance from his father and has passed on a wonderful legacy.

Dad saw in his father qualities that are becoming increasingly rare in our society: dependability, faith, self-sacrifice and humility. My father embraced those same qualities and allowed them to define his life. The inheritance he received became his own legacy.

Thanks to the choices of my grandfather and my father, I can look at what God has brought into my path and truly say:

> LORD, you have assigned me my portion and my cup;
>   you have made my lot secure.
> The boundary lines have fallen for me in pleasant places;
>   surely I have a delightful inheritance. (Psalm 16:5-6)

WE PASS ON A LEGACY

Inheritance is poured into us; legacy pours out from us.

Every man holds this concept deep in his heart. All of us have two primary needs: the need for *intimacy,* safe, genuine relationships with other people; and the need to make an *impact,* to know that our existence matters.[1]

There is a deep message in our hearts that compels us to influence the world and the lives around us. It is that same message that inspires us to consider the legacy we will leave behind.

Jeremiah 32:18 is both a powerful and disturbing verse. It says, "You show love to thousands but bring the punishment for the fathers' sins into the laps of their children after them." These words are enormously convicting! When I sin, when I'm proud, when I'm short-tempered, when I'm selfish, my sin doesn't only affect me. We fathers pass on those patterns of sin. They are laid into the laps of our children. And our children carry them.

One of the pieces of junk that my family collected is the belief that others' opinions of us determine our value. I allowed myself to believe my worth was primarily based on the impression I made on others. It had better be good.

It's not that my parents, teachers or church leaders specifically said so. But I picked up subtle clues and came to my own conclusion that my value was based on performance. That became an underlying assumption of how I should live my life.

Sadly, that message didn't remain just with me; it became a piece of junk I passed on to my kids. My daughter, Barclay, is a wonderful woman, but when she was a little girl she was a blonde handful of determined energy! She was affectionately known at Sunday school as the "White Tornado."

One evening, the board chair for the ministry I worked with came for dinner. The house looked wonderful, the kids were behaving. Every family member was doing a great job of making a good impression on this important man.

After we finished dinner the kids went upstairs while I carried on a conversation with my friend. Soon I noticed a commotion going on; the kids were starting to race around, playfully yelling at each other. So I said, with infinite patience, "Excuse me, Bob. Hey, kids, calm down up there. You need to be quiet."

About thirty seconds of quiet passed and then the yelling began again. A second time I interrupted our conversation and called up to the kids, with a bit more intensity this time. "Kids! Dad said to be quiet, so please obey." About twenty more seconds of silence passed, then, they were yelling back and forth again.

Finally I realized there was no more hiding it—Bob now knew the truth about me. I was not able to control my own children! I got up from the table, "Excuse me, Bob," I said with a forced smile, "I've got to take care of something here."

I went upstairs appearing calm and collected, but as soon as I got to the top of the stairs I saw Barclay running out of my son's bedroom screaming. Something snapped. I grabbed her, lifting her up off the ground, went into my bedroom and threw her down on the bed. I looked directly into her eyes, hovering inches over her face, and with all of the rage behind my embarrassment I hissed at her, "You keep quiet! Don't you *ever* disobey me when we have company!"

I never came so close to striking one of my kids in anger as I did that night. This was my daughter, whom I love, yet I exploded at her.

I left her lying on the bed—terrified—and returned to a polite conversation with Bob over my wife's outstanding carrot cake. Barclay kept quiet.

Something was profoundly injured in my daughter that night. I demonstrated to her that Daddy is not always safe. To this day, every time I'm reminded of my behavior my eyes fill with emotion.

Later that evening as I thought through my reaction, I asked myself, *What was that all about? That was a piece of junk, Craig. You just proved your conviction that you must impress others at all costs. Nobody, not even your daughter, is going to expose you as being less than competent.*

I might as well have looked my daughter in the face and said to her, "Don't you dare show anybody that we're not a perfect family! Don't reveal the truth about us!" I needed this man to think well of me, even at the risk of my own daughter's spirit. What a tragedy!

Later I apologized to her and let her know I had acted wrongly. Of course, she immediately forgave me, as little girls do. But the damage was already done. I had unwittingly exposed a deeply held belief—"I must appear competent"—that in fact was a wound. That wound had never been healed, transformed. As a result it became part of the legacy I passed on to Barclay.

She too struggles with the same overconcern with the opinions of others. In a recent conversation with her she described past and current relationships where she spent a lot of her time making sure friends were happy. "I was hurt by them a lot and often very afraid of making them upset. It became more about what they thought of me than having a true friendship," she said.

Fortunately, she sees herself making progress in that area through the support of her wonderful husband and a deeper understanding of how God actually views her: He loves her to death. She also let me know, "You've come a long way too, Dad." Whew!

That's what happens with the junk we collect. If we are not transformed, if we don't allow other men and women, our church community and the Holy Spirit to work in us, we'll pass on the same wounds of the inheritance we received.

The good news is that God *is* at work transforming us. We are no longer just natural descendants. We are now children of God. Yes, our sins are laid in the laps of our children, but we are now no longer trapped in old sin patterns; we belong to a new family. God himself now works in us and transforms us into a reflection of his grace.

The miracle that has taken place in the spiritual condition of Christ followers is so dramatic that we are called new creations (2 Corinthians 5:17). Our hearts have been changed, and they continue to be changed. Spiritual maturity is an ongoing journey of living out the transformation of our hearts. With humility and dependence on God's Spirit living within us, those changes can and do happen.

First Corinthians 16:13-14 is a transformational passage for men. It begins, "Be on your guard; stand firm in the faith; be men of courage; be strong." On the surface those words look pleasing to the male eye. They charge us:

- Be vigilant.

- Be resolute.

- Be valiant.

- Be mighty.

This verse calls us toward attributes that fit the picture we've always had when we think of manliness. But there is a hidden surprise here that is the key to male transformation: verse 14, "Do everything in love." I beg your pardon?

Having charged us with a noble calling that we find inspiring, if somewhat unreachable, this passage asks more of us: do all of these things in love.

How do we do that? We can only answer that question by looking at Jesus' example in Scripture. Among other passages, Philippians 2:5-11 demonstrates that Jesus humbled himself and gave himself up in love for others. Unlike our own, his inheritance was one of power and authority. Yet, though he had the nature of God, he confined himself to the limits of flesh; going further, he took on the nature of a servant; further still, he allowed himself to be executed by the most painful and degrading means known at the time.

Jesus' inheritance was unique; he was vigilant, resolute, valiant and mighty—like no other man in history. Yet he passes on a legacy of humility and sacrificial love. He looked nothing like the pseudo-role models our culture worships: men who use their strength to control others, revealing true weakness; men who use risk-taking courage for selfish gain and the accrual of reassuring possessions, revealing their fear; men whose strutting demand for respect is a smoke screen for an insecure identity.

Whatever our inheritance, the key to transforming our legacy is to follow the path Jesus took. He pursued humility and rejected all that was self-serving. His heart and mind were directed to the care of others. That became his legacy. That can be ours as well.

Men who use their strength and courage for the sake of others focus on faithfulness, dependability, compassion, sacrifice. The direction of all of those attributes is outward—toward others. None of them are self-directed. The man who pours himself out pours a Christlike legacy into the lives of all he touches.

The transformation of our inheritance into a legacy is not a result of performing and striving. It's a result of brokenness. It's coming to the end of myself and confessing, "If it's up to me to work harder, strive more and perform better, it's just not going to happen." It's realizing, "Lord, I simply need you to transform me." The miracle of God's grace is that he actually does.

Transformation Determines Our Legacy

If we want to repeat the wounds of our inheritance, we can do that on our own. We can pass on anger, fear, weakness, selfishness without any effort. In fact, it's because we make no effort that those qualities do get passed on.

But if we want a godly legacy, we must pursue genuine community. We need relationships where we tell each other the truth and "spur one another on toward love and good deeds" (Hebrews 10:24), where we believe the best in each other and cheer each other on. That is where transformation takes place.

One of the greatest lies men believe is, "I'm the only one who feels what I feel, the only one who struggles with what I am tempted by." I used to believe that my fears and flaws were unique to me. No one else struggled with them. It has taken a while, but I have come to realize that this belief is a lie.

The fact is that we men need a safe place to share the truth about ourselves, because we all struggle with the same issues. We need men who are willing to listen to us, identify with us and not judge us. We need brothers.

Proverbs 27:17 says, "As iron sharpens iron, so one man sharpens another." Each scrapes off the corrosion from the other, making both brighter and sharper. Without the interaction and support of other men, we deal with our pain and anger the way we always have:

- We become controlling and destructive in our family relationships.
- We comfort ourselves with alcohol and drugs, sexual fantasy and acting out gratification.
- We bury ourselves in the success and affirmation of the workplace.
- We withdraw emotionally and become passive.

We're familiar with these patterns. They are part of the inheritance and legacy of many men. We see them in other men, and they see them in us.

Not long ago, I met a man who experienced profoundly the consequences of living in isolation. He was part of a small group, meeting with several other men on a weekly basis. This man, whom I'll call Jack, shared with the group some of the struggles he and his wife were having in their marriage, as well as work expectations that were requiring him to travel frequently. Predictably, the more Jack traveled, the worse his marriage became.

Over time, Jack attended the group less frequently and he began to pull away. One of the men in the group was getting periodic updates on how things were going in Jack's marriage. There was distance, silence, conflict—all the traits of an eroding relationship.

Eventually, Jack disconnected himself from these men entirely. Due to busyness, travel, embarrassment or ambivalence, Jack didn't respond to any requests to meet with the group or the leader.

A year later the leader was amazed to get a call from Jack. When they met over coffee, he revealed that he had not only pulled away from his wife and the men's group, but that he had abandoned his relationship with God. Living largely in isolation, Jack dove into a sexual affair with one of his out-of-state female business contacts.

He went on to describe a bone-chilling experience. Feeling alone, distant from God, estranged from his wife and kids, and isolated from his "soul friends" in the men's group, Jack decided to end it all. Late one night, he bought a heavy-duty rope and a bottle of Jack Daniels and drove to the empty parking lot of a nearby shopping center. Jack tied one end of the rope around the base of a lamppost in the parking lot. He ran the other end through the back of his hatchback to the front seat and tied it into a noose. He slipped the noose over his head, tightening it around his neck.

His plan was to draw courage from the bottle, start the car and floor it. When the car reached the end of the rope, Jack's problems would be over.

Unexpectedly, Jack passed out before finishing the bottle. He woke up the next morning half-seated in his car, half-lying on the parking lot. In a clearer frame of mind, he realized that this was no solution to the pain of his isolation. What he needed was a realization of God's abiding love for him, a recognition of the deep value of his relationship with his family and a reminder that there are friends who stick closer to each other than brothers (Proverbs 18:24).

It was during this time of marriage conflict and the temptation of an illicit relationship that Jack *most* needed other men—men who were committed to reminding him what he really believed and what his calling in life truly was. Apart from these kinds of friendships, all men are eventually capable of turning down a path similar to Jack's.

It has been said that in isolation we are known by our weaknesses; in community we are known by our strengths. The darkness and secrets of isolation reinforce our worst habits; the light of authentic community defeats the power of sin, allows others to support us and one day invites them to lean on us.

Our legacy is transformed by the power of community. When we love others enough to enter their lives and humble ourselves enough to allow them to enter ours, we become changed. The depth of that engagement with others determines what kind of legacy we will pass on.

The two most important decisions in life—determining our relationship with Christ and creating our legacy—are rooted in grace. In his profound reinterpretation of the writings of Thomas à Kempis, Bernard Bangley says this about what is truly important in life:

> Human nature wants recognition. It wants admiration for good deeds. But grace hides its good works and private devotion and gives all praise to God.
>
> Such grace is a heavenly light, a gift from God. It is the mark of a truly spiritual person. As nature is restrained, grace increases, and the soul becomes stamped with the image of God."[2]

As our nature is restrained, our soul becomes "stamped with the image of God." In working toward a meaningful legacy, we must allow God to transform us; otherwise we will most assuredly pass on the same self-centered convictions and wounds of the inheritance we received.

The truly significant life is not about accruing possessions, wealth, acclaim, power and position. It's about grace, compassion and forgiveness. It's about community, servanthood and courage. These are the attributes that define a legacy that will live forever; all of them are directed to the benefit of others.

As I consider the inheritance I received, beginning in the soil of Northern Ireland that nurtured the lives of my grandfather and his ancestors, I have found a growing appreciation for historical prayers of blessing. One such prayer, of Saint Benedict, speaks to the spirit of submission that invites a journey of transformation:

> Almighty God, give us wisdom to perceive you,
> intelligence to understand you,
> diligence to seek you,
> patience to wait for you,
> vision to behold you,
> a heart to meditate upon you,
> a life to proclaim you;
> through Jesus Christ our Lord,
> who lives with you and the Holy Spirit,
> one God now and for ever.
>
> Lord, be with us to guide us,
> within us to strengthen us,
> without us to protect us,
> above us to raise us,
> beneath us to uphold us,
> before us to lead us,
> behind us to guard us,
> ever about us,
> this day and evermore;
> this day and evermore.

May we invite the guidance of the Father's hands upon our lives to transform the legacy that we leave with others—this day and evermore.

12

TRANSFORMATION ACROSS THE LIFESPAN

ONE MAN'S JOURNEY

James Houston

Having nine grandchildren, most of them now in their twenties, I have often longed to tell them, in just ten minutes, the basic hard lessons I have had to learn myself about wise living. But unfortunately I think faster than I can act, and I act faster than I have character to change. If these lessons have taken me over half a century to learn, they won't be imparted by speed reading!

There is a Confucian saying that it is easier to move mountains or to divert rivers than it is to change the human personality. Conversion narratives can attest to remarkable experiences of transformation, and yet at the end of a long Christian life, we can regret that we had not changed enough. Conversion is basic to the Christian life, but we are called to make ever more sacrifices, ever more dying unto the Lord Jesus, that the life of Jesus also may be seen in us (2 Corinthians 4:10).

As we consider the transformation of our character, then, we face two questions, not one: How do I become a Christian? and How do I live as a Christian?

HOW DO I BECOME A CHRISTIAN?

I was once on an international commission to study the environmental perceptions of natural hazards. We studied the San Andreas fault in California and to our surprise found that situated on the fault were five hospitals, the headquarters of the Red Cross and the house of a prominent geologist!

The "fault line" of our inner dispositions varies as widely as our unique narratives and may be so concealed that we are unaware of their effects on our behavior. For example, a child may have been conditioned to perform well, but it was never explicit what this meant. From pregnancy some may inherit undisclosed anxieties or the sense of evil spirits or proneness to addictions or the fear of abandonment. Others may trace broken relationships back to a lack of early bonding or to a lack and then a fear of intimacy or to inarticulate anger.

Living under such hidden pressures can have catastrophic consequences later in life: a performance-conditioned child may grow up endlessly "fixing things," being authoritarian, legalistic and dogmatic, and showing other evidences of inner rigidity, fear, and anxiety. Some may put up a smokescreen of humor to avoid allowing others to read their soul. There are countless compensatory forms of behavior we can adopt, many of which even bring us success in the eyes of the world, and yet they can be death-giving.

As Jesus read the heart of the rich young ruler, he could say, "one thing you lack." So too we may need the courage to know this basic lack within our inner lives. As we resign our efforts to redeem ourselves through the vain efforts of pseudo-transformation and come under the authority of Jesus, we experience the redemption of our Redeemer.

Being a Christian is thus a dynamic possibility—once become, to become yet more so. This was expressed by Johann Arndt in his book *Of True Christianity:* "Adam ought to die in us, and Christ to live: . . . It is not enough to know the Word of God; for if we know it, it must also be expressed in our whole Life and Practice."[1]

How Do I Live as a Christian?

Conversion is thus basic to the Christian life, but its potentials of change remain more poetic than realistic, because human beings are complex creations, and change must contend with that complexity. We possess a temperament, develop a character and relate with a personality.

Our personality is perhaps best associated with our relations with other people. I can see dramatic changes within my own life, perhaps most obviously my becoming less ambitious and competitive over the course of my eight decades. One learns that to live with clenched fists in defiance of other people is likely to give one a heart attack. As I have cultivated the spiritual value of gentleness and "the exercise of self-abandonment to divine providence," as a seventeenth-century French writer described it, my self-consciousness in how I conduct my relationships has changed over time, leading to better health and a gentler outlook.

Our temperament is most closely associated with our body. Some people are naturally intense and highly spirited; others are relationally warm-hearted and relaxed. Still others are seemingly always angry and aggressive, or easy-going, careless, even depressed. In the ancient world these distinctions were associated with "humors" in the body, of blood and bile conditions. Wrong as these medical conditions may now be specifically known, the distinctions are still real: they are the hardest conditions of our life to ever to change significantly. A type-A person tends to remain that, whether as a street gangster or as an evangelist.

Our character involves our worldview and our ethics. It is developed consciously through spiritual exercises, or less consciously in the establishment of moral convictions. Our professions can shape our character like the discipline of a pilot or the reliability of a teacher or the compassion of a nurse. Thus we can conceive of character formation as deliberate efforts to become a responsible moral agent primarily in the day-to-day experience of life.

SPIRITUAL HONESTY AND HUMILITY

We need, therefore, to be realistic and modest about our claims for transformation. Indeed, if our transformation is a genuine expression of God's grace, we actually become more aware that we remain sinners. So our prayer becomes more frequently that of Cyprian: "Lord forgive me in my good actions."

Recently at a youth camp I was impressed by the common desire expressed—to grow in godliness. Yet I could not help reflecting, perhaps even such a noble desire should not be too self-conscious. As a young friend confided recently to me: "I am tired of baby-sitting my own personality." For even a desire to grow in godliness could deflect us from carrying out more immediate human tasks of just seeking, under the lordship of Christ, for "a genuine human existence."

Only the mediated relationship of the God and Father of our Lord Jesus Christ by the ministry of the Holy Spirit can redeem us; when we project on God the dysfunctional relationships we have had or our compensatory responses, then our view of God is readily distorted.

For example, if you were taught to always obey unquestionably ("yes sir," "yes ma'am"), is it not natural to be drawn to the commands in the Bible while overlooking the covenantal love of God, assuming that our relationship with him is ordered by the rule "I obey therefore I relate"? One can, of course, react in the opposite way, so that the least sniff of authority and the Bible is closed. A person can be so profoundly lonely as a child that he or she develops an intense companionship with God, so that such a person is either cut off from the rest of the human race or too spiritually arrogant to penetrate.

It is a sober thought therefore that having a devotional life, or being engaged in ministry, are not enough in themselves to be transformed into Christlikeness. Introspection and "religious activity" can only go so far.

Perhaps we are viewing ourselves too detachedly instead of relationally. Perhaps we need to be more relaxed in God's love. Perhaps God does look after us better than we do ourselves. Might it help to be more "in

Christ" and less in ourselves? Should we live less tensely if our way of life is being more unconsciously self-forgetful, with a relaxed playfulness, a good sense of humor and a deep trust in divine friendship?

A Relational Reformation of the Church

There is another caveat about transformation I want to make. Living as persons in an impersonal universe has become the greatest contemporary challenge to our whole world today. As Christians, we can be self-centered even as we praise the Lord for our transformation! As postmodern society dissolves further into individualism and narcissism, we need to emphasize more than ever that Christian maturity is corporate—not individualistic.

So much in our relationships is driven by doing things that give us gratification and *inadvertently* bring us into conflict with others. Our motives for social contacts and relations vary widely. Some people are nurturing and altruistic in guiding, encouraging and accepting others, but some of us are ambitious, assertive and controlling of others, using them as our own personal resources. Some are adhesive, needing companionship and being flexible and adaptable to others, just to belong. Some need others always to affirm how right they are in their judgment, or indeed to excel over others in their competition with them. Some need to have an audience to exhibit how they can act judiciously, to assert their authority or wisdom, provide expertise and strategic leadership. Again others are more of a mix of motives, cautious, conscientious, supporting, seeking others to grow and to become as independent as those they admire. Some are always fighting for principles, while others are always protecting the underdog.

We might even overdo our perceived strengths so that we receive negative responses instead. A teacher needs to be always right. A manager must control. Even a kind person can be overly kind, while an honest person can be too blunt. These can become the most intense conflicts within a Christian community.

Thus more than ever, we have need of a "relational reformation of the church." Our relational wounds, received relationally, can only be healed relationally. We can test our gracious transformation most critically by the shift from *What's in it for me?* to how, instead, I see my relations with others are becoming more deeply redemptive, bringing Christian joy into other people's lives. Our prayer should be that of Francis of Assisi: "Lord, help me not so much to be understood, but to understand; nor to be loved, but to love; for it is in the giving that we receive." Indeed, it is in the healing we seek for others that we become healed ourselves.

CHRISTIAN LIVING ACROSS THE LIFESPAN

I have sought to live by a principle first expressed by the classical philosophers: knowledge without action is meaningless, and action that does not foster friendship is useless. To live in a relational universe as a person in the triune God of grace means that human relationships have priority over all other actions and thoughts. As such, Christian life is much more tested in the home than in the church. I have often reminded my students that their academic degrees are a much less significant statement about their Christian life than the look on their spouse's face!

Our lives are where our faith is formed and tested; therefore we can observe patterns in the challenging events which shape our lives that suggest a practical theology for a transformed and transforming life. For instance, I've learned over time and by experience that people matter more than institutions. Self-interest, as Jesus observed in the scribes and the Pharisees, can make institutional life appear to be very proper and yet very wrong! Officialdom can become so inflexibly self-interested that it is assumed to be always right, whether determined by expediency or for the good of the institution, and is left without the willingness or even ability to repent of mistakes or of wrong-doing.

There follows from this a second costly principle: Personal transparency matters more than political or professional self-protection. I learned from one of my professors, an evangelical leader of Hungary during the Nazi and then communist occupation of his country, that being wholly open about one's way of life, even to one's enemies, is far more protective than the half lies, concealment and other forms of fearfulness that move us to hide ourselves. Personal transparency is the courage to place oneself in the hands of God, wholly so. Learning to overcome my fear of what other people may think of me was a great step forward into the freedom to be selfless and to express myself.

The apostle Paul's affirmation: "seeing then that we have such hope, we use great plainness of speech" (2 Corinthians 3:12 KJV) became a wonderful mandate for me to have transparent relationships. Of course, I have needed to learn gentleness and to gain the discernment of how much reality others may be able to tolerate. But I learned from William Gurnall, the Puritan saint who expounded in over fifteen hundred pages his "short commentary" on Ephesians 6:10-20, that to "put on the whole armor of God, is to have no self-defences."

But this fosters another choice of values, of faithfulness over success. For there can be no category of success in dealing with human relationships. Approachability, openness, empathy, kindness, loyalty, gentleness, the inadequacy of the self without the other: all help to generate a transformative way of life that personalizes where otherwise there would be alienation within an impersonal world of things. Indeed, Ignatius of Loyola calls on us in his *Spiritual Exercises* to be indifferent to all creaturely things for the supreme worship of the Creator of all things, since in him "we live and move and have our being" (Acts 17:28).

Therefore "offer your bodies as living sacrifices, holy and pleasing to God—this is your spiritual act of worship" (Romans 12:1). Having walked a long path of being transformed through such living sacrifice, my present life is filled with joy and contentment, surrounded by a family who all love the Lord and are engaged in service for him. I feel like the old knight sculpted on a tomb near the high altar in the cathedral of

Uppsala, Sweden, that I once saw. He is lying at rest on his marble bed, being stripped by flying cherubs of all his armor, now no longer needed. The battle scars are healed, the campaigns are all behind him. In self-abandonment to divine providence, he is at peace.

NOTES

Chapter One: Transformation

[1]Henri Nouwen, *Letters to Marc* (New York: HarperCollins, 1998). p. 74.

Chapter Two: The Spiritual Journey

[1]Kallistos Ware, *The Orthodox Way* (Crestwood, N.Y.: St. Vladimir's Seminary Press, 1979), p. 7.

[2]Richard Byrne, "Journey," in *The New Dictionary of Catholic Spirituality,* ed. Michael Downey (Collegeville, Minn.: Liturgical Press, 1993), p. 568.

[3]In Acts 9:2; 19:9, 23; 22:4; 24:14, 22 the Christian faith was simply known as "the Way."

[4]Bernard of Clairvaux, *Collected Works,* trans. G. R. Evans, (New York: Paulist, 1987), p.102.

[5]Janet Hagberg and Robert Guelich, *The Critical Journey* (Salem, Wis.: Sheffield, 2004).

[6]Dallas Willard, "Live Life to the Full," accessed December 20, 2005 <www.dwillard .org/articles/artview.asp?artID=5>. I recommend Dallas Willard's books *The Spirit of the Disciplines* (San Francisco: HarperSanFrancisco, 1991) and *Renovation of the Heart* (Colorado Springs: NavPress, 2002).

[7]Francis de Sales, cited in *Devotional Classics: Selected Readings for Individuals and Groups,* ed. Richard Foster and James Bryan Smith (San Francisco: HarperCollins, 1993), p.29

[8]Andre Louf, *Spiritual Classics: Selected Readings for Individuals and Groups on the Twelve Spiritual Disciplines,* ed. Richard Foster and Emilie Griffin (San Francisco: HarperSanFrancisco, 2000), p. 32.

[9]C. S. Lewis, *Prince Caspian* (New York: Macmillan, 1951), p.136.

Chapter Three: Intimacy with God

[1]William Cowper, "There Is a Fountain Filled with Blood" (1771).

Chapter Four: The Past

[1]Richard Rohr, cited in Gordon Dalbey, Sons of the Father (Wheaton, Ill.: Tyndale House, 1996), p. 9.

[2]Walt Disney's popular animated movie The Lion King makes the point engagingly. Pioneer Weldon Hardenbrook also detailed it in his 1987 book Missing from Action: Vanishing Manhood in America (Nashville: T. Nelson, 1987).

[3]Jeffrey Zaslow, "Julian Lennon on His Dad—and His First Disc in Seven Years," USA Weekend, May 28-30, 1999, p. 22.

[4]John Whitcomb, Great American Anecdotes (New York: William Morrow, 1993), p. 21.

Chapter Five: Failure

[1]Henri Nouwen, "Moving from Solitude to Community to Ministry," Leadership Journal, Spring 1995.

[2]Thomas Merton, quoted in Ron Rolheiser, "Key Elements in Therese's Spirituality," accessed December 20, 2005, <www.ronrolheiser.com/key_elements.pdf>.

[3]John Calvin, Institutes of the Christian Religion, 1536 ed., trans. Ford Lewis Battles (Grand Rapids: Eerdmans, 1995), p. 15.

Chapter Six: Vocation

[1]Fil Anderson, Running on Empty: Contemplative Spirituality for Overachievers (Colorado Springs: Waterbrook, 2004), pp. 3-4.

[2]Tom Stella, The God Instinct: Heeding Your Heart's Unrest (Notre Dame, Ind.: Sorin, Books, 2001), pp. 123-24.

[3]Brother Lawrence, The Practice of the Presence of God (New York: Harper & Row, 1941), p. 29.

[4]Ibid., p. 23, emphasis added.

[5]Joan Chittister, Wisdom Distilled from the Daily: Living the Rule of St. Benedict Today (San Francisco: Harper Collins, 1991), p. 83.

[6]Ibid., pp. 85-86.

[7]Frederick Buechner, quoted in Ken Gire, Windows of the Soul: Experiencing God in New Ways (Grand Rapids: Zondervan, 1996), p. 71.

[8]Parker J. Palmer, Let Your Life Speak: Listening for the Voice of Vocation (San Francisco: Jossey-Bass, 2000), p. 2.

[9]Ibid., p. 3.

[10]Martin Buber, *Tales of the Hasidim: The Early Masters* (New York: Schocken, 1975), p. 251.

Chapter Seven: Friendships
[1]C. S. Lewis, *The Four Loves* (London: Fontana, 1960), p. 62.

[2]Thomas Moore, *Soul Mates* (New York: HarperPerennial, 1994), p. 21.

Chapter Eight: Sex
[1]Tommy Nelson, *Book of Romance: What Solomon Says About Love, Sex and Intimacy* (New York: Thomas Nelson, 1998).

[2]Brennan Manning, *Ruthless Trust: The Ragamuffin's Path to God* (New York: HarperCollins, 2000), p. 16.

[3]C. S. Lewis, *Till We Have Faces* (New York: Harcourt Brace, 1984), p. 308.

Chapter Ten: Parenting
[1]Behavior modification used in these parenting models often masquerades itself using the terms *Christian, spiritual, God's way* and *wise.*

Chapter Eleven: Legacy
[1]I'm indebted to Larry Crabb for his insights about human needs on the deepest levels. See his book *The Marriage Builder* (Grand Rapids: Zondervan, 1992), p. 29.

[2]Bernard Bangley, *Growing in His Image* (Wheaton, Ill.: Harold Shaw, 1983), pp. 62-63.

Chapter Twelve: Transformation Across the Lifespan
[1]Johann Arndt, *Of True Christianity,* trans. A. W. Boehm (1712), p. xliv.

CONTRIBUTORS

Fil Anderson is executive director of Journey Resources, based in Greensboro, North Carolina. He is a frequent speaker at conferences, offers individual spiritual direction and directs retreats and workshops around the country. Fil worked with Young Life for twenty-five years, serving as area and regional director before becoming national director of training. He is the author of *Running on Empty: Contemplative Spirituality for Overachievers.*

Howard Baker teaches spiritual formation and spiritual direction at Denver Seminary and Fuller Seminary, Colorado. When not running, skiing or road tripping with his wife, Janis, Howard serves as a spiritual director to pastors, seminary students and Young Life staff. He is the author of *Soul Keeping* and a contributor to the Renovaré Spiritual Formation Study Bible.

D. Ross Campbell started his medical career operating a hospital for Wycliffe Bible Translators in Bolivia. He is the author of *How to Really Love Your Child, How to Really Love Your Teenager, How to Really Love Your Angry Child, The Five Love Languages of Children* (with Gary Chapman), and numerous other books.

Gary D. Chapman is president of Marriage & Family Life Consultants,

Inc., and has served on the pastoral staff of Calvary Baptist Church in Winston-Salem, North Carolina, since 1971. His books include *The Five Love Languages* series, *Covenant Marriage, The Four Seasons of Marriage* and *The Other Side of Love: Handling Anger in a Godly Way.*

David G. Benner is Distinguished Professor of Psychology and Spirituality at the Psychological Studies Institute in Atlanta, Georgia. A psychologist, spiritual director and retreat leader, Benner has written and edited many books including *Surrender to Love, The Gift of Being Yourself* and *Desiring God's Will,* and is an executive editor of the journal *Conversations.*

Gordon Dalbey's first book, *Healing the Masculine Soul,* helped to pioneer the Christian men's movement in 1988 and was followed by *Sons of the Father: Healing the Father Wound in Men Today* and *Fight Like a Man: Redeeming Manhood for Kingdom Warfare.* A popular speaker at conferences and retreats around the world, he has appeared on Focus on the Family, The 700 Club and many other radio and TV programs. He lives with his wife and son in Santa Barbara, California.

Robert A. Fryling is publisher of InterVarsity Press and vice-president of InterVarsity Christian Fellowship, where he has worked for thirty-five years. With his wife, Alice, he has coauthored *Handbook for Engaged Couples, Handbook for Married Couples* and *Handbook for Parents.* Bob speaks regularly on issues of leadership, spiritual formation and the intersection of faith and culture.

Ken Gire is the author of many books, including *Windows of the Soul, Moments with the Savior* and the Reflective Living series. He and his wife, Judy, live in Monument, Colorado.

Craig M. Glass is the founder and director of Peregrine Ministries, which offers individual coaching, small group teaching, retreat speaking and guided adventure for men to leave a lasting legacy with those they love. Craig and his wife, Beryl, live in Monument, Colorado, and have three children, Barclay (married to Vincent), Alec and Conor.

James Houston is founding principal, former chancellor and emeritus professor of spiritual theology at Regent College in Vancouver, British Columbia. He is the author of some forty books, including *I Believe in the Creator, The Transforming Friendship, In Search of Happiness, The Heart's Desire* and *The Mentored Life*.

John D. Pierce lives in Charlotte, North Carolina, where he serves on the ministry staff of The Barnabas Center. His professional attention is directed toward group ministry to men and their families, particularly in the realm of sexuality, intimacy and addiction. He is a nationally certified, licensed professional counselor. He shares life with Sandy, his wife, and is the proud father of Drew, Carlee, and Catherine.

Stephen W. Smith is cofounder and spiritual director of Potter's Inn, a Christian ministry devoted to the work of spiritual formation through soul care, spiritual direction, guided retreats, art, books and study guides. Steve pastored churches in North America and Europe for over twenty years prior to founding Potter's Inn with his wife, Gwen. They now travel extensively offering ministry to churches, groups and missionaries. Steve is the author of *Embracing Soul Care: Making Time for What Matters Most* (Kregel, 2006) and *Soul Shaping: A Practical Guide for Spiritual Transformation* (available through www.pottersinn.com). He and Gwen reside in Colorado and have four sons.

Doug Stewart is national coordinator for spiritual formation with InterVarsity Christian Fellowship. He and his wife, Marilyn, offer retreats, courses and spiritual direction in the United States, and around the world. They live in Wheaton, Illinois, and have three daughters and four grandchildren.

Potter's Inn is a Christian ministry founded by Stephen W. and Gwen Harding Smith, and is dedicated to the work of spiritual formation. A resource to the local church, organizations and individuals, Potter's Inn promotes the themes of spiritual transformation to Christians on the journey of spiritual formation by offering

- guided retreats
- soul care
- books, small group guides, works of art and other resources that explore spiritual transformation

Steve and Gwen travel throughout the United States and the world offering spiritual direction, soul care and ministry to people who long for a deeper intimacy with God. Steve is the author of *Embracing Soul Care: Making Space for What Matters Most* (Kregel, 2006) and *Soul Shaping: A Practical Guide to Spiritual Transformation.*

Potter's Inn at ASPEN RIDGE is a 35-acre ranch and retreat nestled in the Colorado Rockies near Colorado Springs, CO. As a small, intimate retreat, Potter's Inn at Aspen Ridge is available for individual and small group retreats. "Soul Care Intensives"—guided retreats with spiritual direction—are available for leaders in the ministry and the marketplace.

For more information or to for a closer look at our artwork and literature, visit our website: www.pottersinn.com

Or contact us at
Potter's Inn
6660 Delmonico Drive, Suite D-180
Colorado Springs, CO 80919
Telephone: 719-264-8837
Email: resources@pottersinn.com

TRANSFORMATION OF A MAN'S HEART *SERIES*

The Transformation of a Man's Heart series puts men in conversation with God and with one another to see how God shapes us in the ordinary experiences of our lives. The book, featuring reflections on the masculine journey by experts in a variety of fields, can be read independently or in concert with the four discussion guides, which look in depth at the role of sex, marriage, work and transformation in the spiritual lives of men.

Each guide has six sessions, suitable for personal reflection or group discussion and based on essays in the book *The Transformation of a Man's Heart*.

SEX

For all the attention we give it, sex remains a mystery. This discussion guide by Stephen W. Smith and John D. Pierce looks at sex as part of a man's transformational journey and explores how our sexual story can inform our understanding of God and his love for us.

MARRIAGE

This discussion guide by Stephen W. Smith and Gary D. Chapman demystifies marriage for men, helping us see through the euphoria that led us to marry and the disillusionment that plagues us when our marriages don't turn out as we planned.

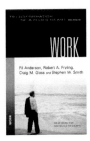

WORK

This discussion guide by Stephen W. Smith, Fil Anderson, Robert A. Fryling and Craig Glass puts men's vocational lives—their calling, their failings, their inheritance and their legacy—into the context of their relationship with God.

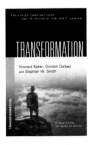

TRANSFORMATION

In this discussion guide by Stephen W. Smith, Gordon Dalbey and Howard Baker, men will be reminded that wherever they find themselves, God is there with them, inviting them out of their woundedness and onto a new and better path.